HOPE LIVES

A Journey of Restoration

Amber Van Schooneveld

Foreword by Wess Stafford

Group

LOVELAND, COLORADO
www.group.com

Hope Lives: A Journey of Restoration

Copyright © 2008 Amber Van Schooneveld

Visit our Web site: **www.group.com**

Credits
Senior Developer/Editor: Roxanne Wieman
Chief Creative Officer: Joani Schultz
Copy Editor: Daniel Birks
Art Director/Cover Designer: Jeff A. Storm
Book Designer/Print Production Artist: The DesignWorks Group
Sr. Project Manager: Pam Clifford
Production Manager: Peggy Naylor

Photos courtesy of Compassion International.

Unless otherwise noted, Scripture taken from the HOLY BIBLE, NEW INTERNATIONAL VERSION®. Copyright © 1973, 1978, 1984 by International Bible Society. Used by permission of Zondervan Publishing House. All rights reserved.

Library of Congress Cataloging-in-Publication Data

Van Schooneveld, Amber, 1978-
    Hope lives : a journey of restoration / by Amber Van Schooneveld.
      p. cm.
    ISBN 978-0-7644-3847-9 (pbk. : alk. paper)
  1. Poverty—Religious aspects—Christianity. 2. Christian life. I. Title.
    BV4647.P6V36 2008
    261.8'325—dc22   2008000290

10 9 8 7 6 5 4 3 2   17 16 15 14 13 12 11 10 09 08
Printed in the United States of America.

Table of Contents

WEEK 1: THE POVERTY OF THE HEART 9

The first step on the journey is to understand the poverty of the heart, to search our hearts and ask why it's sometimes so hard to help those in need. How are things like materialism and individualism stifling compassion? On the journey, we'll set down the burden of guilt and pick up God's grace instead.

WEEK 2: GOD IS NOT SILENT 47

God has provided a map for our journey in loving others. This week we'll explore what the Bible has to say about serving the poor, the widows, and the orphans, and how God desires for us to show his love to those in need.

WEEK 3: UNDERSTANDING POVERTY 81

Understanding poverty will guide the steps we take in releasing others from it. This week we'll explore what poverty is—its causes and effects and how it's a spiritual matter at its core.

WEEK 4: PRAYER 117

Prayer is the weapon God has given us for the journey of loving and serving those in need. This week of prayer and journaling will help us explore the power of prayer in a world in need of restoration and help us make prayer a part of daily life.

WEEK 5: BE THE CHANGE 151

The journey of serving those in need is, in essence, the journey of following Christ. And God has created each person uniquely for the journey, giving each one spiritual gifts, skills, and passions with which to serve him, to be the change we want to see in the world. This week we'll explore our individual gifts and be reminded that it is God's grace that sustains us along the way.

Foreword

"There will always be poor people in the land." I've thought about this Scripture from Deuteronomy 15:11 for years.

The verse haunted me throughout my years growing up among the poor on the desolate plains of the Ivory Coast in West Africa. It taunted me each time I witnessed the death of a childhood friend from malnutrition, diarrhea, or another preventable disease that cut life short in that area of the world. "Why," I asked, "does poverty exist? Why, on earth, are we doomed to see it always?"

Even with that biblical edict, I became a crusader against poverty. For more than 30 years now, I've dedicated my life to fighting poverty and its effects upon its smallest victims: children. Emboldened by my childhood experiences and fueled by my desire to protect these little ones, I have committed my life to combating the mind-set of the poor that often says, "You don't matter. Just give up."

It breaks my heart to hear good people lament that they also want to do something about poverty but don't know where to begin. They honestly don't know what to do or whom to trust! But as I recall how I became an advocate, a "doer" in the fight against poverty, I realize there's another reason many Christians may not get involved with the poor: *If you don't know the poor, it's hard to serve them.*

As president of Compassion International, I lead an army of child advocates who live to serve the poor. And everything I need to know to guide this global ministry I learned around the campfires of my poverty-stricken village in West Africa.

The poor taught me about love, joy, and generosity. Living among them and serving them taught me about patience and relationships. Working beside them taught me about courage, strength, and incredible faith.

Hope Lives challenges us as Christians to focus on becoming what God is calling us to be. This book demands that you interrupt your busy life and embark on a spiritual journey to know the poor through God's eyes, through his words. Through this journey, you will understand why God values the poor and why he repeatedly asks us to serve them. It is my greatest desire that this book will help you develop a deeper relationship with God and, in doing so, ignite a natural response and a passion to serve the poor as God directs.

"There will always be poor people in the land." Yes, the poor will always be with us. Which gives us all ample opportunities to serve and, as a result, grow closer to God.

—Dr. Wess Stafford
President, Compassion International

Introduction

"He has showed you, O man, what is good.
And what does the Lord require of you?
To act justly and to love mercy
and to walk humbly with your God."

—MICAH 6:8

Each morning before I start my day, I turn on my laptop, sit on my couch, and browse through the news. The stories I read make it hard to believe in hope. Stories of staggering poverty, stories of overwhelming numbers of AIDS victims, stories of communities gutted and raw from war, stories of children exploited and hungry and discarded. I close the laptop and sit. Overwhelmed and paralyzed. Overwhelmed by the enormity of the problems. Paralyzed by not knowing what to do.

And yet, I serve a God of hope. A God of love. A God of healing.

Where do I, where does the God of hope, fit into this confounding world around me?

Sick of sitting on the couch, I went on a journey to find out. And I've found that hope lives.

I stuck my nose in the corners of the world and peeked into crannies, and found that hope is very much alive. Our God of hope is on the move to bring restoration to me and to you and to this world full of hurt.

He's calling each of us on a journey of restoration with him. Hope lives, and God is on the move.

This book will be a continuation of God's journey for you, as you take each step of your life following Christ. Each week for the next five weeks, you'll begin a new stage of the journey. Five days each week you'll read a short chapter and then reflect on it, journal, and pray.

Princess Diana had it right: "You can't comfort the afflicted without afflicting the comfortable." The first week of the journey starts as a journey of affliction—of boring down into ourselves to find out why we're still on the couch, overwhelmed and paralyzed instead of comforting the afflicted. We'll explore materialism, individualism...all the "isms" that keep us from caring about poverty. It hurts to look at ourselves raw and exposed, but God will use this self-scrutiny to heal.

The journey continues in the second week to the Scriptures, the clear path God has drawn for us to love what he loves; to feed those who hunger, break the chains of the oppressed, and protect the orphan; to follow and become more like Christ. God will reveal his heart for this world and for you through his Word, and he will transform you by it.

The next step of the journey is a closer look into poverty and the issues plaguing the world—what are they, and what in the world do they have to do with us? God will use this week to prepare us to know how to react and act in this world of need.

Step four of the journey is a week of prayer—a week learning of God's incomparable power through prayer for this world, and a week of humbling ourselves before God, asking for his healing and preparation as we set out to answer his call to love our neighbor.

The last week of the journey, God will reveal to you the special ways in which he has created you *just exactly so* to be his messenger of hope, love, healing, and service to those in need.

Above all, this is a journey toward Christ, a journey compelled and enabled by grace. It's not a journey of guilt or obligation. It's a journey of God's grace restoring us to the people he created us to be, and a journey of serving God to bring his grace and love to those in need. Jesus Christ, who has called you a friend, will be walking by your side, while the Holy Spirit guides and transforms you.

God is inviting you on a journey with him. Pray that he will guide and plan every step of your path as you act justly, love mercy, and walk humbly with your God.

The Poverty
of the
HEART

THE FIRST STEP on the journey is to understand the poverty of the heart, to search our hearts and ask why it's sometimes so hard to help those in need. How are things like materialism and individualism stifling compassion? On the journey, we'll set down the burden of guilt and pick up God's grace instead.

ere on earth
you will have many

Margaret

because

the worl

DAY 1: TRIALS AND ABANDONED TREASURES

"Here on earth you will have many trials and sorrows. But take heart, because I have overcome the world."

—JOHN 16:33 (NEW LIVING TRANSLATION)

At first, Margaret thought the cries she heard were just her imagination. She was in a remote area. Only poor farmers ventured into this stinking, swampy plot of land to satisfy their thirsty animals. It certainly wasn't a place she liked to go and was no place for a child. Yet, there they were again: shrill, panicked cries.

Margaret had raised nine children; still she had never heard a cry of pain like this. Just up ahead the grandmother saw her goats nudging a small straw basket that lay mired in the mud. She peered inside. The infant was naked, her skin crusted in mud and blood. As the baby wiggled, Margaret could see dark, finger-shaped bruises on the child's neck. Suddenly the grim reality of the scene became apparent. There was only one reason a mother would bring her child to this desolate spot. Only one reason why a nurturer would turn murderer, wrapping her fingers around her own child's neck.

Margaret reached inside the basket and picked up the abandoned baby girl. Her wrinkled hands softly patted the child's back until her cries faded to shaky gasps. Margaret began the long walk back into town, her stooped body curved protectively over the child in her arms. Though covered in mud, blood, and disease, the baby Margaret had found was an abandoned treasure. Margaret named the child Deborah—and this grandmother of six became a mother again.

Deborah was constantly sick. Margaret didn't need to take her to a doctor to know that she had AIDS. She had seen enough children in her village die to know. She also knew that, without a job, she could never afford the medical care Deborah needed. Margaret loved Deborah, but she knew she couldn't care for her. She found a neighbor to take Deborah in. *She's been abandoned again,* thought Margaret as she walked away from Deborah's cries. But Margaret determined to check on Deborah often.

One day she found Deborah tied to a tree like a dog. Ignored. Neglected. Shaking with anger, she untied the crying child and took her home. She hadn't rescued Deborah from the swamp to abandon her to abuse.

Deborah's health continued to worsen. Some days, when the sick child lay weak and crying, Margaret regretted her decision to walk toward the cries she had heard on the day she found Deborah. She couldn't handle watching this child die. In those moments of desperation, Margaret felt a twinge of empathy for Deborah's birth mother. That poor woman couldn't face watching her daughter die—a nightmare that Margaret was living each day.[1]

Jesus warned that on this earth we'd have trials and sorrows. Sometimes I can't help but think that's a major understatement. Even as I read it, I know Deborah's story is just one among thousands…among hundreds of thousands. There are 1.2 billion people in the world living in extreme poverty on less than a dollar a day. There are 38.6 million people diagnosed with HIV worldwide. There are nearly 30,000 children under the age of 5 dying each day of hunger and preventable diseases. There are stories of abuse, neglect, and evil that freeze my heart and stories of stupid, senseless poverty that bewilder my mind. There are countless children like Deborah—a little treasure knit together, inch by inch, by God—slowly undone by disease, poverty, and abuse. And no matter how much I want to forget that these numbers represent real people, I know that each one of the nearly 30,000 children is a story of a treasure. A diamond God crafted to catch and reflect his light just so, but now kicked in the dirt, muddied, unrecognized, and abandoned.

This is such a harsh, messed-up world…and I don't know how to take it. I want to throw up my hands and accuse God or someone or something. Of course, the Bible has never shied away from the state of this world. The first son born to man murdered the second one, and famine and disease are as old as Abraham. Indeed, this world is fundamentally broken and won't be fully fixed in our lifetime. I read the stories each day. Stories of unthinkable genocide and cruelty, tribes wiping out entire tribes. Stories of pandemics crippling entire nations and erasing generations. Stories of children given little opportunity at life before being sold as slaves or stolen as soldiers. Stories of babies whose lives were forfeit from the start, without nutrition, clean water, or care.

On the Other Hand

But on the flip side, I'm experiencing a very different story unfolding. The stories I see on TV stay in that little box—they don't invade *my* world. My section of the world is living through unprecedented prosperity, safety, and opportunity. Advances in technology, industry, trade, education, and law have created a bastion of opportunity.

1   Adapted from a story by Brandy Campbell, Compassion International.

Sure, I grew up pinching pennies, but I was always well-fed; it was always an expectation that I would go to college, get a good job with health benefits, buy a house. Far from the despair reigning in certain pockets of the world, my industrialized world and I are thriving. We have more material wealth than any other generation in history. I drive down the street and see huge hospitals and hulking high schools; I see homes squatting like hotels; I see megacorps and megamalls and megachurches. My church buddies and I are thriving, too—we have our many church meetings, our building campaigns, our community outreaches playing Frisbee at the park with Starbucks afterward.

Put simply, we are prospering. But never able to leave well enough alone, I still can't help but wonder, as I sip Starbucks on an easy Sunday afternoon: Is this pleasing God? Is *this* his vision of what his world should look like?

Looking at God's Word, I see it isn't the first time the question has been raised. The nation of Israel, in the time of Isaiah the prophet, faced a similar question. The people of Israel were a good people. In some ways they were like me. In many ways they were better. They were pious, keeping up their religious practices. They were prosperous, enjoying the fruits of their righteous nation. They were well-intentioned, regularly seeking God. And they very rightfully asked God, "Does this not please you?"

So when I read the words God said to them through Isaiah, they hit me like a linebacker.

Raise Your Voice

Shout it aloud, do not hold back.
Raise your voice like a trumpet.
Declare to my people their rebellion
and to the house of Jacob their sins.

For day after day they seek me out;
they seem eager to know my ways,
as if they were a nation that does what is right
and has not forsaken the commands of its God.
They ask me for just decisions
and seem eager for God to come near them.

"Why have we fasted," they say,
"and you have not seen it?
Why have we humbled ourselves,
and you have not noticed?"
Yet on the day of your fasting, you do as you please
and exploit all your workers...

Is this the kind of fast I have chosen,

only a day for a man to humble himself?

Is it only for bowing one's head like a reed

and for lying on sackcloth and ashes?

Is that what you call a fast,

a day acceptable to the Lord?

Is not this the kind of fasting I have chosen:

to loose the chains of injustice

and untie the cords of the yoke,

to set the oppressed free

and break every yoke?

Is it not to share your food with the hungry

and to provide the poor wanderer with shelter—

when you see the naked, to clothe him,

and not to turn away from your own flesh and blood?

—Isaiah 58:1-3, 5-7

I can't help but make the comparisons…these Israelites' religious lives sound a lot like mine. They went to Temple every day. They devoted themselves to learning about God. They prayed faithfully. OK, so I don't go to church every day. But when I read this, I see myself and so many Christians I know—eager for God to come near, attending church meetings several times a week, reading the Bible faithfully, and taking classes on getting to know God more.

But God was not impressed with the Israelites. And I'm not sure he is pleased with my religiosity either. I can't help but ask, "Why not, God? Don't you see how much I'm doing for you? Don't you know how busy I am for you? Haven't you seen my acts of worship—fasting and praying? He answers,

"Is that what you call a fast, a day acceptable to the Lord?"

It is a crushing moment.

What *does* God want from me, from his people? What is true fasting, true religion? God says it is this: "to share your food with the hungry and to provide the poor wanderer with shelter—when you see the naked, to clothe him." And James gives me another clue: "Pure and genuine religion in the sight of God the Father means caring for orphans and widows in their distress" (James 1:27, NLT).

Feeding the poor, caring for the oppressed…that's messy stuff. But what if what God wants is messy? What if, like the Israelites, my spiritual service is a bit too tidy? a bit too contained in the white walls of religion? a bit too focused on me? What if all this time I've been polishing myself up to exhibit spiritual excellence—like it's some precious jewel—when what God really wanted was something wholly different? Not to stay home perfecting myself, but to go out into the world. To transform it through action, in service and in love. Honestly, leading a Bible study and fasting sounds a whole lot easier. But when I read those passages again, the conviction doesn't go away. God is calling his people—me—to do something different. To refresh and restore this world full of Deborahs.

Margaret found God's abandoned treasure, Deborah. She picked her up, brushed her off, and made the hard choice not to ignore her plight, but to love her. I think God may have treasures waiting for me to help him restore, a journey he's calling me on to be his light in a dark world.

Margaret woke up from her nightmare, the nightmare of watching Deborah slowly die, the day she heard that a local church was opening a program in her village. The program would provide health care, nutritious food and supplements, spiritual guidance and education, and the loving embrace of a local church. Deborah was the first child to be registered.

Because of the program, Deborah's medical bills were covered, as well as the extra food she required. Her health has improved, and this once abandoned, sickly infant is now an active 4-year-old who loves to play house with her favorite doll. She is now in a child sponsorship program, with a family sending her letters of encouragement and love and sharing Jesus' hope with her.

Margaret struggles to express her thanks to those who have given life to her daughter. "I don't know what to say," says Margaret, her voice choked with emotion. "Thanks to the staff and the church, Deborah can get care. Without their support I wouldn't have made it this far."[2]

---

2   Adapted from a story by Brandy Campbell.

In My Own Words

What about Isaiah 58 challenges you?

Why are you reading this book? What interests you
about it? What are you hoping for?

MY PRAYER

God, I want to begin a journey with you. My past religious activity seems to
have left something out…it seems to have been a little too much about me.
Thank you that you want to restore my soul to be like yours. Thank you that you
want to take me on a journey to become your hands and feet in this world that
needs you. Help me to follow you and become like you.

DAY 2: BARELY GETTIN' BY: THE LIES OF AFFLUENCE

"I come from the Marcy projects, in Brooklyn, which is considered a tough place to grow up, but [visiting Africa showed me] how good we have it. The rappers who say, 'We're from the 'hood,' take it from me, you're not from the 'hood."
—RAPPER JAY-Z, REFLECTING ON A TRIP TO AFRICA

"Give me neither poverty nor riches!
Give me just enough to satisfy my needs. For if I grow rich,
I may deny you and say, 'Who is the Lord?' "
—PROVERBS 30:8-9

You are rich. I'm not speaking metaphorically or spiritually. I mean it: You're rich. If you're reading this book right now, you're most likely among the financially elite in the world and in history—even if you're from a low-income household in America. Did you drink clean water today without risk of death or disease? Are you wearing a pair of shoes? Do you have a dry, safe place to sleep tonight? Did you eat today? You are rich. You are richer than billions of others. The Gross National Income per capita in the United States in 2003 was $37,610. In India it was $530. In Ethiopia it was $90.

I think an interesting phenomenon is occurring. So many of us—myself included—honestly think we're just barely getting by. I'm just living my modest life, trying to pay my bills…but it's just not true. *I am living the "good life."* I mean, I take showers every day if I feel like it. I can buy foreign spices to season my food. I see movies on Saturdays. I'll buy a $4 coffee with whipped cream if the fancy strikes me.

But I still often feel like I'm the poor one around here. I live in an apartment next to an area where the average home cost is $600,000. Going from my one-bedroom apartment to see the glorious mansions I'm surrounded by, I feel like maybe someone ought to be giving *me* money. It's easy not to feel rich as I drive down the road in my hand-me-down Chevy when I'm surrounded by Lexus SUVs. But if I were cruising in New Delhi, my Chevy would be looking pretty good.

Rich Fool

The saddest thing about me driving discontentedly down the road in my Chevy, not realizing that I'm rich, is that I honestly sometimes believe I really don't have the extra money to help others. I've reclassified my luxuries to necessities, and there's just not any "unnecessary" cash left over for others. My dinners out, my Frappuccinos, my third red sweater, my trip to the beach, my DVD collection—those are part of my necessary budget. I work hard; I deserve them. They're not luxuries…

I've read all the verses about treasuring money, how it's easier for a camel to go through the eye of a needle than a rich man to enter the kingdom of God. But I always think it's someone else who's treasuring riches. Not me. I honestly don't think I'm the one with a problem around here. But if I, if rich America, doesn't have a problem with riches, who does? Who is it? Who in the history of the world has been as comfortable as 21st-century America? I'm not talking about my neighbor with that fancy new car. I'm not talking about my co-worker who's always getting her nails done. I'm not talking about my friend who's always buying the newest CD. I'm talking about me. *It's me.* I'm the one trying to jam my bulging camel's hump through the eye of a needle. I need to wake up. I am the rich fool.

THE AVERAGE PERSON in the United States gives only 2.1 percent to all charitable causes. The average Christian in America tithes 2.66 percent of his or her income to the church. If we assume that Christians are also giving the additional 2.1 percent of their income to charitable causes, that's still only 4.76 percent of their income—not even half of the biblical tithe (Leviticus 27:30-32).

More

My wealth, America's wealth, is our god, and it is blinding us, deluding us, suffocating us. The standard of living in America is constantly on the rise. I don't just enjoy the wealth I have; it makes me hungrier, constantly on the prowl to get more and more. I get one thing, check it off the list, and move on to the next. There's a hierarchy of possessions in America, and we march toward checking off each next thing on the list. The new phone technology. Check. A new car. Check. A new home. Check. A new boat. Check. On and on we march in an unending quest for material achievement, driven by possessions.

And I'm stuck in the drudgery of the march, my possessions a thick sludge I'm wading through. The more I get, the more I want, piling up thing after thing. One more toy for the entertainment center. One more sweater. Soon the sludge has swallowed my ankles, then my knees; soon I can't walk. Eventually I'm paralyzed—trapped in a big pile of stuff, my arms pinned to my sides, unable to reach out and help anyone else.

"Our mobile society encourages competition and economic aggression rather than contentment. Someone who isn't climbing the social ladder is regarded as a fool and a failure. We're taught to climb to the top of the heap. What we're not taught is that the heap is a garbage heap."

—PETER KREEFT,

BACK TO VIRTUE

Gross National Income per Capita 2003 (U.S. Dollars/Atlas Method)	
Switzerland	$39,880
United States	$37,610
Japan	$34,510
United Kingdom	$28,350
Mexico	$6,230
Egypt	$1,390
India	$530
Bangladesh	$400
Kenya	$390
Ethiopia	$90

Source: World Bank, "GNI per Capita 2003," World Development Indicators database (New York: World Bank, 2004).

Ice Cream, Cheese, and Books on Poverty

I like to think of myself as a generous person. I like to think of myself as a frugal person. I also sometimes like to think of myself as a poor person. If you look at my (and my husband's) finances for one month, you'll see that I'm really quite a deluded person.

Income after taxes and health insurance:		$2204.32
Rent:	$800	
Boring bills:	$308.23	(phone, energy, car insurance, etc.)
Tithe:	$250	
Groceries:	$215.87	
Savings:	$107.60	(I know, I know, I should be saving more.)
Two designer sweaters:	$84.26	(They were on clearance; I couldn't resist!)
Two purses:	$80.67	(My husband convinced me I needed two.)
Charitable donation:	$75	
Dinner out:	$68.50	(We went to this fabulous restaurant in town.)
New game for the Wii:	$50	
Gifts for family:	$41.45	
Fast food:	$36.16	
Books about poverty:	$32.94	(I need to be informed, right?)
Ice cream:	$22.67	
Cheese:	$20.41	(I have a thing for cheese and ice cream!)
Movies:	$10.56	

This is more embarrassing than I thought it was going to be. I don't usually buy two purses. I swear. This particular month was an expensive month—my husband was graduating with his master's; I was going on a trip and needed a new purse. I'm usually more reasonable…but it's always something, isn't it?

In *one month alone*, I spent nearly as much on ice cream, cheese, and books on poverty as the average person in Ethiopia makes in *one year*. Who's rich now? I spent more on *one meal out* than a person will make in Haiti in *two months*. Who's frugal now? I spent almost *three times* as much on cute sweaters (in May) and purses and a video game as I did on charity to help others. Who's generous now? I invested about 3 percent of my money in helping others. I spent about 15 percent on luxuries for myself.

I'm not condemning myself for eating that dinner out or buying those purses. I'm under God's grace. But I need to have my eyes open wide to the choices I'm making and stop believing that I'm just barely getting by and really can't do much to help others.

What Do I Want to Do?

My favorite rock star, Bono, remembers growing up in Ireland being in awe of America. When we walked on the moon, he remembers thinking, "Wow, these Yanks are crazy." And still today as an adult, he says, "Part of me is still that child with his mouth open at this great idea called America…with the surety that there's nothing you Americans can't do if y'all want to do it. In the 21st century, what does America want to do?"

What *do* I want to do?

I don't have to be paralyzed by stuff. I'm resourceful. I'm hard-working. And most of all, I'm commissioned by God to use my power, resources, and love to reach out to the poor and oppressed in the world.

And I don't have to be paralyzed by the seemingly insurmountable problems of the world. Nothing is insurmountable to God, and after all, it's God who is telling me to reach out.

Even if I can change just *one* life, give hope and comfort and love to one person, that would be a tremendous, significant, celebratory act. That would be one person who perhaps Jesus has wept over, one person the angels will rejoice over, and one more treasure of God, just like Deborah.

So, 21st-century America, what do we want to do?

What do you spend your money on in any given month?
How could you designate a percentage to help others?

MY PRAYER

Dear Lord, thank you for blessing me with comfort in this life. Thank you for the roof over my head and the food on my table. Thank you that you want to bless me and give me good gifts. But I have become blinded by my wealth, not seeing it for what it is. Please help me to daily appreciate the blessings you have given me. Help me not to be tightfisted with them, but to open my hands to share with others as well. I want to be a steward of my wealth to help others. Please guide me as I seek to do this.

DAY 3: THE GOOD LIFE: MYTHS AND MISTAKES OF THE AMERICAN DREAM

"Perhaps many dreams have been fulfilled – a move to a larger house, to vice president, to a condo after the kids have finally moved out – but the soul has become like a boarded-up discount store in an empty parking lot with weeds rising up out of the pavement cracks."

—DAVID L. GOETZ, *DEATH BY SUBURB*

"And what do you benefit if you gain the whole world but lose your own soul? Is anything worth more than your soul?"

—MATTHEW 16:26 (NLT)

Let me start with this: God bless America. I've lived abroad, and I love this place. I love our indomitable spirit that spurs us to realize our dreams. I love our frank honesty. I love our foot-long Coney dogs. And God certainly has blessed America—we enjoy relative safety, prosperity and hope, and the footprints of Christ can be seen in our sense of justice, our desire for equality, and our love of the little guy.

The American dream is alive and well, the dream of the good life. I see it around me—in my friend who started her own dog-biscuit business and in my country-bumpkin friend who became a doctor. I think of them and remember the immigrants who streamed here looking for a life of choice and possibilities. And I like to think that when these immigrants first saw America they "held [their] breath in the presence of this continent…face to face for the last time in history with something commensurate to [our] capacity for wonder."[3] The American dream is the dream of each person—the wonder at what could be if we were just given opportunity. A desire for a life of freedom, happiness, and prosperity.

I see how far we've come and how the American dream is really the hope of each heart…but still I wonder whether it has drifted from its original glory. I look at my life and wonder.

3   *The Great Gatsby*, F. Scott Fitzgerald.

I wonder if we've forgotten it. Sometimes it seems as if the once noble pursuit of the American dream has diminished—diminished into a selfish and busy grab for the good life.

It's All About Me

"A self-sufficient human being is subhuman."
—ARCHBISHOP DESMOND TUTU

I saw a girl recently wearing a T-shirt that said, "It's all about me." How cliché that's become—I barely noticed the words because they're so ingrained in my American mind-set. And though I can judge that girl for her tactless T-shirt, I have to admit, Burger King's slogan that I can have it "my way" pretty much sums up how I'd really like to live my life. I'm plied with media messages that it's all about me, that I should have what I want…and I eat it up.

America *was* founded on individualistic ideals, but the cliché "it's all about me" is relatively new. It has only recently become commonplace to embrace and even brag about self-centeredness. I certainly wouldn't have caught my grandmother in that T-shirt. Her generation, living through the world wars and the Great Depression, far from being "all about me," was necessarily dependent on one another. The spirit of her day was to realize the American dream of prosperity and freedom and justice by helping one another. I relish stories my mom tells of my grandmother, whose community banded together to survive the Great Dust Bowl in Kansas. And my great-great-uncle, who bought a milk truck during the Depression to give milk and bread to the children who otherwise wouldn't eat. And my great-grandmother, whose parents couldn't afford to take care of their many children, so a neighbor took her in and cared for her.

I have been blessed to always have my needs taken care of…but I've never had to rely on my community like this, in such an in-person, hands-on, self-sacrificial way. My material comfort has made me immune to this kind of dependence. And I have to wonder, what am I missing?

Double Pickles

In modern-day America, the individual is king. Don't misunderstand—I'm so glad I live in a place that affirms the value of the individual—the American ideal of the individual has lent deserved dignity to each created human that other cultures have stripped the individual of. In our culture a human isn't just a cog in a machine or an indistinguishable drop in the ocean of humanity. Every single person has a purpose, a role to play. But sometimes it seems like this concept has bloated to grotesque proportions, the concept that we individually have value having ballooned to the idea that the individual is paramount, that my needs and wants are of utmost importance. I see it in my understanding of rights: *I* have the right to be comfortable. *I* have the right to look out for my own interests. *I* have the right to a Quarter Pounder, hold the mayo, with double pickles. It's all about me, me, me.

How did the American dream turn into this? I have the freedom to be an individual that few in history or across the world today have had. In my grandmother's genera-tion, with each rationing food and pitching in, a person with an "all about me" atti-tude simply wouldn't have been tolerated. But today I have enough to hide in my little corner apartment, shut my door behind me, and turn on the air conditioning—relying on no one and solely looking out only for myself.

Today I took a drive down a remote mountain road. My car overheated, and I pulled off to the side and put up my hood. About 10 cars passed by on this narrow, quiet moun-tain road before one elderly couple pulled over to see if I needed help. That convicted me. I've passed lots of stranded motorists in my day, thinking, "I'm sure they're OK. They probably have a cell phone; they can take care of themselves. *I don't want to get involved.*" My "take care of myself" attitude has isolated me—I don't reach out. And so my mind-set that what really comes first is myself reigns supreme. I think, "I'd like to help her with her family problems, but I've just got so much on *my* plate right now." And "I know that family needs financial help right now, but I've got to take care of *my own* business first." *It's in these small thoughts that my individualism wins out over Jesus' love for the poor, breeding my neglect of others.* I've slowly and subtly accepted the lie that helping myself first is wise, justified, and just good sense.

I look at what my attitude has become and, though I don't want to, I can't help but think of this verse: "You must have the same attitude that Christ Jesus had. Though he was God, he did not think of equality with God as something to cling to. Instead, he gave up his divine privileges; he took the humble position of a slave" (Philippians 2:5-7, NLT). I really don't want to be a slave. In the same breath, Paul tells me what my attitude should be: "Don't be selfish…Be humble, thinking of others as better than yourselves. Don't look out only for your own interests, but take an interest in others, too" (Philippians 2:3-4, NLT). My good sense in thinking of myself first and not getting involved in the needs of others is, simply put, unchristian and disobedient.

Subhuman

A quote by Archbishop Desmond Tutu asserts that a self-sufficient human being is subhuman. Subhuman. According to this Christian African man, the way I, and many

Americans, sometimes live our lives—largely independent from one another, just taking care of ourselves—makes us *less than human*. How rude! I want to argue. But his words cut like a knife.

I think of a particular friend. She was one of those "problem people." She always seemed to be in trouble—late rent, missed meetings, lost jobs. It was messy to be her friend. I don't like messes. So I swept her under the rug. I smiled and offered to pray and ignored her needs. I didn't help. *Subhuman*. My stomach turns over. Memories of those moments I chose to ignore her needs, to live sufficient unto myself in my tidy world, make my stomach lurch. I didn't do what I was created for. I was, in my humanity, diminished—a broken creation, gathering dust on a shelf, not doing what it was made to do.

A part of my soul is missing and broken when I'm not connected in the bond of human need. I need the humility of those in need. I need their sacrificial hearts. I need their love for others. I could learn far more from them than it's comfortable to admit. Without them, I am "a boarded-up discount store in an empty parking lot with weeds rising up out of the pavement cracks." My cracked soul needs God's grace and healing.

Busy, Busy, Dreadfully Busy

My individualism really isn't quite enough to stop me from helping the poor around me. But I've managed to create just the right combination, a one-two punch, to keep my love stifled: individualism coupled with busyness.

I can remember so many conversations past: "How's your week going?" "Oh, it's great, but I'm *so* busy. I have meetings every night this week and a presentation to give Friday." "Oh, I know. I've got so much to do this week, too." This conversation could be heard on any college campus, in any church meeting, on any soccer field, in any grocery store across the country.

"Busy" is our banner. And I think we're proud of it. Telling of my myriad responsibilities, I struggle to keep a slight swelling of pride and competition out of my voice as I tick off my list.

We've got soccer practice, choir practice, Pilates, MOPS, church on Sunday, church on Wednesday, overtime, swim meets, board meetings, and band practice. Our lives are full. We are up to our necks in activities. And what's left, our heads, we fill with iPod, iPhone, Wii, TiVo, *Survivor*, and *American Idol*. That's it. We're full up. We're constantly moving, and when we're not moving, we're pumping our brains full of information or stimulation. Every second of the day. There's simply no room for anything else.

And it seems that, as with individualism, our busyness sprouted from virtue. Americans are industrious. We believe in responsibility, in excellence. We believe in working hard to provide the best life possible for our families. We are a great nation, in part, due to our work to achieve more than our parents did. But has our drive slowly warped into something ugly? Has our industriousness turned to selfish ambition?

We're always pushing ourselves to do more, to work harder. But why? I see it each week on the reality TV show (that I won't actually admit to watching) where husbands trade wives. Week after week, you see men who started with good intentions—men who just wanted to provide for their families—but have become trapped in the busyness of the business world. They push themselves to work more, work harder, work later, to move on up, to beat the Joneses, but they neglect their families in the meantime. I myself do it. I'm driven. I'm always achieving. I'm keeping myself busy, running, moving up and on. I want to do good with my life. But sometimes I think it's just this whip of achievement at my back that keeps me running—that keeps my fellow Americans running. To achieve great things, to be better than the next person, running a brutal race toward ever-expanding goals.

All busyness isn't bad—I know people who work their brains out to provide for their families. Hard work isn't the problem. But there's this itch to constantly be moving and achieving—overfilling our lives, overfilling our brains, and moving up the financial ladder, the social ladder, the sports ladder, the career ladder, and even the spiritual ladder.

We've hit the maximum capacity of what our bodies can do with our time and what information our brains can process. When one more thing comes flying at us—for example, a plea to help the poor—it hits a wall. There's just not room for it in our brains or time for it in our lives. We want to help, but we've just already got so much going on. We don't have time to think about it. We don't have time to care about it. At the most, we quickly scribble a check, toss it in the mail, and keep running.

I think of how Jesus lived. I've heard many a sermon on what a busy man Jesus must have been. I'm not so sure about that. He had many demands pressing in on him from every direction, but he wasn't busy in the same way we are. He wasn't running from meeting to meeting or from practice to practice. He very well might have spent many nights sitting with a group of friends over dinner, lingering for hours and hours, just talking about life. By today's standards, that might even be called lazy and self-indulgent. But what mattered to Jesus was people—listening to them, loving them, and helping them. He was busy with the slow work of taking time to care for people. He was never too busy to stop and help someone.

I want to be like that. But in my dreadfully busy life, I hear myself singing along with that VeggieTales song in the story of the Good Samaritan: *Busy, busy, dreadfully busy...Much, much too busy for you.* I don't have the time to stop and help. It's an interruption to my schedule, not the focus of it as it was for Jesus. Like a good individualist, I think first of my own priorities and what I need to get done, and there are few scraps of time or thought left over for the poor.

I want to be like Jesus. I don't quite know how or where to start, but I know that this is his journey. I know Christ is leading me and healing me and making me more like him.

How have you seen individualism and busyness negatively affect other people's ability to help others? How has it affected you?

How can you overcome a tendency to not get involved in others' lives? to stay too busy to help?

MY PRAYER

Dear Lord, I praise you and thank you for this country where you've placed me— for the opportunity and safety and hope I can have here. Thank you for all the blessings I have here. Please help me not to turn my industriousness into selfish busyness. Help me not to let my all-about-me attitude persuade me to neglect those you want me to reach. I want you to transform me to be like Jesus. Thank you for your Holy Spirit who helps me.

DAY 4: WILLING IGNORANCE AND GUILTY CHARITY

"Very often we know enough to choose not to learn more lest we feel guilty...Rich Christians know enough about the ravages of poverty that we turn off the TV special on poverty... We know that knowing more will make us morally obligated to change."

—RONALD J. SIDER, *RICH CHRISTIANS IN AN AGE OF HUNGER*

"Remember, it is sin to know what you ought to do and then not do it."

—JAMES 4:17, NLT

Several years ago, I lived in the beautiful city of Amsterdam, known for its grand architecture, bright tulips, and...prostitution. Prostitution is technically legal in Amsterdam, as whatever is done behind closed doors is considered to be your own business. Thus, the red light district is a series of rooms with large windows facing onto the streets. Women stand in the windows, scantily clad and advertising their wares. You knock on the door, and what happens behind the closed door is your own business. That was about all I knew about it.

One day I walked home with a friend, past the chocolate shop and the grand church I passed each day. She told me about an experience she had had the day before. She had been walking down the crowded narrow canal streets near the red light district, and a woman, walking in the opposite direction, pressed a note into her hand as she passed by. And the note said this:

Help me. I'm being held as a prisoner, forced to be a prostitute. Me and four other women are kept locked in a room. They force us to prostitute, and they won't let us out.

The woman, being escorted, brushed past my friend on the street, and she never saw her again. I was dumbfounded hearing this story. It was absurd. Here I was, walking in the European sun, peering into the windows of the chocolate shop, and somewhere in this civilized city, women were locked in a room and raped? "No way," I thought. "It can't be true. It sounds like one of those Internet stories." I didn't know what to think. It was too horrible to be true, and if it were true, what could I do anyway? Overwhelmed and confused, I shut my mind. I chose not to believe this tall tale. I did nothing. I moved on.

In the next several years, stories like this started popping up wherever I looked. Magazine articles about girls from Thailand kidnapped and forced to become prostitutes. Reports on Eastern European women lured to Amsterdam and America with the promise of a job and then imprisoned. I slowly began to realize that it was true. That desperate woman that day in Amsterdam had cried out for help, trusting a random stranger on the street to help save her. It fell on deaf ears.

I will never forget that woman on the street in Amsterdam, how I chose to stay ignorant, to close my mind, and do nothing. *I did nothing.*

Do You Shudder?

I wonder how many of us are living numb in a state of willing ignorance. We hear so much. So many stories of death. So many statistics of despair. So many pictures of grief. Sometimes I wish there were no Internet or long-distance communication so that all I'd have to worry about is my own little town. I'm overwhelmed. I don't think God created me to take in this much despair. My brain just can't keep processing these statistics: 1.2 million children are trafficked each year as slaves; 854 million people are hungry today; more than 1 billion live on less than $1 per day. 1.2 million. 854 million. 1 billion. A blur of numbers. I am numb. The words are meaningless. I've hit capacity for caring.

And so I shut down. I've heard one statistic too many, and I just can't take it anymore. As I did on the street in Amsterdam that day, I don't know what to do, I can't quite believe in the problems, so I do nothing. I feel myself developing a protective film that covers my eyes and anesthetizes my heart. If I saw the problems in person, if I looked in the children's eyes, I would shudder. But I only see numbers, not faces.

And I don't shudder anymore.

I stay half ignorant on purpose. I skim the news, not letting myself read too much. I glean enough to seem informed: "Oh, yes, it's just a shame what's going on in Africa." I don't get my heart involved. I stay aloof and in control. Separate.

Because if I let go, if I find out, I know what would happen. I would crack. I would break. I'd look into the ugly eyes of poverty and grasp my head in my hands and shout,

"Why, God, why?" But I can't keep doing that every day. And the bad news just keeps on coming. And I don't know what to do. I can't keep caring and keep being broken.

God, I'm just not up to the task.

God, help me.

I need you. I can't care anymore. I don't want to care anymore. I hear these things, these numbers. I see these children's faces. I see the mothers' hollow eyes that don't even ask for help anymore, and I'm broken. My soul is tired of shuddering.

I'm not you, God. You're infinite—you can keep looking at this world and still love it and still bleed for it. I'm finite…but I know you haven't asked me to be you. You haven't asked me to heal every wound. That's not like you. I look at the way you've ordered the world, and I know you've given me just one little piece, one little corner of the world to care for. I don't have to do it all.

But I need your help. I need your strength, your eyes. I need your love that keeps on loving. Mine has dried up and run out. I need your Holy Spirit to fill me and dwell in me and be what keeps me standing and going and loving when my heart fails. I can't soften my own heart. I need you to soften it.

God, I need you.

Guilty Charity

Sometimes I allow myself to be broken. Other times I don't. And in the times I don't, I turn to my two good old friends to cope with my confused heart: *guilt* and *charity*. I know I ought to be doing something and caring, and I'm filled with guilt. Guilt is a great motivator…in the short run. I quickly whip out my checkbook, write a check to the first organization that seems reputable, and wipe my brow. Whew. That's better. Guilt salved; charity fulfilled.

I have a friend who went to a Christian concert. At the end of the concert, pictures were shown of poor kids and their living conditions. A young guy making more money than he'd ever had before, guilt stabbed at him. His friend sitting next to him said, "I'll do it if you do it." Led by guilt, he wrote that check. But guilt doesn't last. It drifts away like smoke, and soon his guilt faded. God can turn our poor motivation to good—my friend now is dedicated to serving the poor. But guilt is not the point. I don't need guilt; I need love.

Maybe I'm guilty for some ills in the world, maybe I'm not. But I don't think God wants my guilty spirit. I think he wants my repentance, my love. He wants to soothe me with his grace. Grace and love transform, like it did my friend. He started with guilt, but God changed him with love. God transformed him through the Holy Spirit. His heart is broken for this world because of the love of Christ. He loves others because Christ loves him. *That* is lasting. *That* is how I want to be.

I'm overwhelmed by numbers because it was never about numbers. One million, 20 million, 200 million. God didn't create me to care about numbers, and numbers create guilt. Thabitha. Gabriel. Sarath. Lavender. Josué. That's who God cares about. That's who God wants me to love.

Mercy Costs

My charity is less true charity than occasional pity. Giving to "charity," I think of how I'm being oh-so-good. A gold star on my Christian report card. Extra credit. At the end of each term, when report cards are about to be turned in, I write that check and check off my charity box. I move on, oh-so-benevolent, with a clean conscience.

I think I've done something above and beyond my call of duty. I haven't. I'm commanded to help the poor again and again in Scripture. (I think God knew this one would be tough for me to grasp and gave extra hints.) Helping the poor isn't undeserved charity. It's justice. Bono put it well: "This is not about charity in the end, is it? It's about justice...I just want to repeat that: This is not about charity, it's about justice."

I think I'm learning that God's justice, what God commands, is that each of his people would have enough bread to live on day by day and be given enough dignity to thrive. It is God's justice that he has commanded me to give. Not charity. An occasional guilt or benevolence offering isn't what God wants from me. True charity is love. True charity is mercy. And it's not extra credit, not an addendum to my faith. As Christians, it's who we are; it's our essence.

I want God to transform my heart by the Holy Spirit so that I love what God loves, so that mercy naturally flows out of me. I want to show others mercy because it was first shown to me; to offer mercy to others as fellow guests at God's table, not as a benevolent queen offering scraps to beggars at my feet.

God, please give me your heart. True charity, true mercy bleeds. It's not an uninvolved, unthinking check. I know you don't want sacrifices that cost me nothing. "If I gave everything I have to the poor and even sacrificed my body, I could boast about it; but if I didn't love others, I would have gained nothing" (1 Corinthians 13:3, NLT). If I give every last cent, but I don't do it in your love, it's a waste. Mercy is attached to my heart. God, please change my heart. I give it to you. Transform it to love with your love.

"Mercy goes beyond justice . . .
Mercy is costly.
Look what it cost God:
the infinitely precious life
of his own Son."

—PETER KREEFT, *BACK TO VIRTUE*

Have you ever allowed a film to cover your eyes and heart, deadening your heart to the needs of others? Write about it.

MY PRAYER

Dear God, I repent. I want to turn away from my cold charity and my willing ignorance. I repent of how I've allowed myself to not really care, to assuage my guilt with empty acts of charity. I turn toward you and give you my heart. Please heal me with your grace. Please fill me with your Holy Spirit. Please transform me to be like you, to love with your love. Thank you that I know you're just waiting to do this.

Action Step

It's easy to stay uninvolved if we can't actually *see* the people in poverty—see the faces of poverty. Visit this Web site to see the faces of your brothers and sisters around the world who are living in poverty: www.compassion.com/child-advocacy/find-your-voice/photo-essays. Click on the photo essay titled "What Does Poverty Look Like?"

Many times we feel paralyzed because we just don't know enough about the compassionate organizations that exist. Use this Web site to familiarize yourself with these organizations, what they're doing, and how they rate: www.charitynavigator.com.

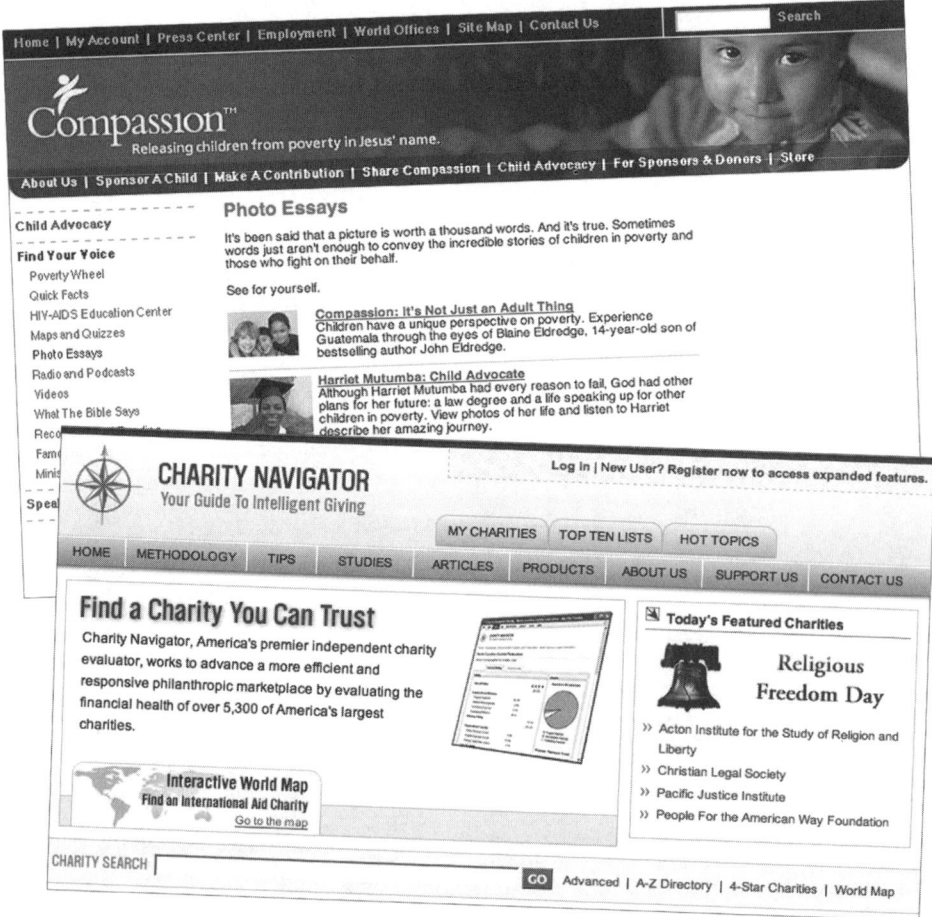

DAY 5: MY BURDEN IS LIGHT

"If I am devoted to the cause of humanity only, I will soon be exhausted...but if I love Jesus personally and passionately, I can serve humanity though men treat me as a door-mat. The secret of a disciple's life is devotion to Jesus Christ."

—OSWALD CHAMBERS

"This is love for God: to obey his commands. And his commands are not burdensome, for everyone born of God overcomes the world."

—1 JOHN 5:3-4

Things I'm learning so far...

1. A life of compassion should be the essence of who I am as a follower of Christ. It's not an addendum to faith or spiritual extra credit for good service.

2. My compassion shouldn't be dependent on how much extra money or time I have lying around. God asks me to help. Period.

3. My compassion should flow from my love of Christ because he loved me first. It's not motivated or sustained by guilt.

4. It's justice God demands in this world for each person. It's not charity or occasional pity I condescend to drop on others. It's justice.

Spiritual Banking

A recent encounter with a small treasure of God convinced me of two more things my compassion can't be. I visited the home of a 10-year-old boy, James, who is HIV-positive. He is such a sweet little boy—soft spoken and gentle with a quiet smile. I put my arm around him as we prayed for him and his family, and his shoulders were so frail I felt as if my clumsy hand could have crushed him. James is undergoing antiretroviral therapy—which will help him grow stronger and prolong his life. He told us of his hope for the future—how he wants to be a doctor so he can help others who get sick.

But sitting next to James, feeling his frailty, I was struck by how there are no guarantees. Antiretroviral therapy is saving many lives, but there's still no guarantee on James' life; he could still die young. And a poisonous thought creeps into my head: "What's the point of helping? Why waste my time when it may not matter in the long run?"

I realize that I'm thinking like a spiritual banker, taking a capitalist approach to my investment in the poor. It's right there in that word: *investment*. In a results-driven society, I can focus on what I (or God's kingdom) am getting out of my investment. What was the outcome of my financial, spiritual, and time commitment? How many were saved? How many were taken out of poverty? How many are living different lives? James becomes some stock I'm investing in—and I regularly check the market to see if my investment is paying off. Yuck.

I know God wants me to be shrewd and wise. I can see from the shrewd manager in Luke 16:1-9 and the parable of the talents in Matthew 25:14-30 that God values those who honestly, intelligently sum up a situation and direct their resources in the manner that reaps the most benefits. *But* my service can't be contingent upon "success." It can't be contingent upon me getting anything in return for my service. Of course I will receive a benefit—in serving others, my soul will probably be changed far more than any I serve—but my payoff can never be the motivation. Jesus gave *everything*, but it didn't always "pay off." Many turn their backs on his grace. But he still gives and loves. I want to love as Christ loved, unconditionally. I want to show Christ's mercy, not make a spiritual investment or deal.

Getting My Fix

The second thing I would never want little James to become is some kind of emotional fix. Sometimes giving to the poor, going on a mission trip, or serving those in need can be like youth-group summer camp. It's a mountaintop emotional high that just really gets me going. It can become a fix.

I have a friend who can relate to this. He decided to visit a little girl he was sponsoring through Compassion International. He'd been exchanging letters with her and was so excited to meet her. He had idyllic, Hollywood visions of their meeting—she'd see him and run to his arms, and they'd hug in the midst of laughter and tears. The reality was a bit different. They met, and she hid shyly behind her principal. He gave her a backpack full of gifts and was so excited to give them to her. She looked at them politely and then zipped the bag back up. It wasn't the beautiful outpouring of emotion he'd hoped for. Years have passed, and he and the girl *have* developed a deep friendship—and he has gotten much emotional "payback" from their friendship. But he knows better than anyone that emotional payoff can't be the genesis of serving. It just doesn't work that way.

Serving isn't about me. I won't always get what I want from it. I will get joy from James' sweet smile, but I may also get pain. I want to love James because God loves him—he is an amazing treasure, and he deserves a chance. Love is the motivator, not the cold calculator of results or the good feelings I'll get.

Not a Burden

There's one thing I certainly don't want as a Christian: one more burden added to my shoulders. It sometimes seems like each week I shuffle to church and learn *one more thing* I need to be doing—a little yellow sticky note posted to my forehead, an external reminder of accouterments I need to add to my faith. Pray more. Read the Bible more. Tithe more. Evangelize more. Serve the poor more. Pretty soon, I'm a mass of yellow sticky notes detailing all the things I need to do to be a "good Christian." But if a strong wind comes up, they're *all* getting blown off.

I don't want to add just one more sticky note to my faith.

If I attach the "good things" I'm supposed to be doing as a Christian as external features, like an additional arm stuck in the side of a Mr. Potato Head, I know it won't be an authentic, lasting change. Sure, I might persevere for a short time under the motivation of guilt or obligation or routine. But my guilt only lasts so long before I resent it. I'll eventually consider my obligation fulfilled. And routines are easy to fall out of. Christ is inviting me instead to be transformed by his love.

"Come to me, all you who are weary and burdened, and I will give you rest. Take my yoke upon you . . . and you will find rest for your souls. For my yoke is easy and my burden is light."

—MATTHEW 11:28-30

The short film *The Shadows of Virtue* is a beautiful exploration of what it means to love the poor and what our motivation in that should be. Check it out at www.humdingerpictures.com.

The Bible's words about the poor aren't my to-do list, another burden on my shoulders. God wants to transform me into a new person. He wants me to find rest in Christ's love. And when my motivation for all things is Christ's love, loving the poor will become an organic shoot growing out of my heart.

I know serving the poor isn't easy; but it's not a burden. It strikes me as one of the great paradoxes of serving Christ. He's blunt about the difficult task of following him: "If any of you wants to be my follower, you must turn from your selfish ways, take up your cross, and follow me" (Matthew 16:24, NLT). Hmm… Crosses are heavy and painful; sounds pretty burdensome. But then Jesus says, "My yoke is easy and my burden is light." How can these two be reconciled?

Dietrich Bonhoeffer's words always give me the shivers: "When Christ calls a man he bids him come and die." I know Christ has asked me to give up my very life to serve him. That could mean any number of things. It might mean I die in the cause of speaking out for the oppressed (as Dietrich Bonhoeffer died speaking out against the wrongs of Nazi Germany). It could mean I give up some comforts in order to help others. It might mean I have to make some difficult business decisions. It might mean I give my time to a widow in my neighborhood. I don't know what Christ will ask me to do. But it might not be easy.

That's why Christ's promise is so sweet: When I'm weary from serving, he will give me rest. I'm simply his servant, carrying out the good deeds he has for me. He isn't asking me to carry the burden of the whole world or fix the whole world or be in charge of making sure everything turns out just right. *He* carries that burden. He asks me simply to love him and love others and act accordingly.

Something happens when a creation does just what it was created to do—it sings. It finds joy and purpose and fulfillment. Far from being a burden in my life, I suspect fulfilling my purpose in loving and serving the poor around me will make me more truly alive. It will nourish me and bring me joy. God is transforming me into his masterpiece—created for the good works he has placed all around me.

And how comforting it is that this is how God promises to take care of me when I spend myself on behalf of the hungry:

Then your light will break forth like the dawn,
and your healing will quickly appear;
then your righteousness will go before you,
and the glory of the Lord will be your rear guard.

Then you will call, and the Lord will answer;
you will cry for help, and he will say: Here am I.
If you do away with the yoke of oppression,
with the pointing finger and malicious talk,
and if you spend yourselves in behalf of the hungry
and satisfy the needs of the oppressed,
then your light will rise in the darkness,
and your night will become like the noonday.

The Lord will guide you always;
he will satisfy your needs in a sun-scorched land
and will strengthen your frame.
You will be like a well-watered garden,
like a spring whose waters never fail.

—Isaiah 58:8-11

In My Own Words

What can you infer from Isaiah 58:8-11 about how
God will help you in serving others?

Week One
Reflection Questions

What was the most challenging truth you've considered this week?

Consider whether material wealth has paralyzed you in the past. What step can you take to ensure your wealth won't block your compassion?

Consider whether you've been living as an individualist—too busy to look to the interests of others. What can you do to live with the interests of others as a priority in your life?

How can you develop a heart for the needs of the world, not allowing yourself to become numb by all the stories?

How can you make sure that your love for the poor is rooted in the love of Christ, not in guilt or obligation?

Action Steps

1. Sit down with your budget and evaluate whether there are luxuries you've been classifying as needs. Consider whether your finances are as God would have them, and where they might need tweaking.

2. Pray through Isaiah 58 several times, asking God to use it to change your heart. Discuss with others what inspires you in the passage.

3. Do one thing this week to help someone in need. It doesn't have to be big:

   • At the grocery store, help a mom with kids carry her groceries to the car.

   • Take extra time to talk to a widow at church to see how she's doing.

   • Take someone who struggles financially out to lunch, or give him or her a gift certificate for a dinner out.

   • If you're with a small group, plan a Saturday morning to help people in your community or church clean their gutters, paint, or do other necessary chores.

God Is Not SILENT

GOD HAS PROVIDED a map for our journey in loving others. This week we'll explore what the Bible has to say about serving the poor, the widows, and the orphans, and how God desires for us to show his love to those in need.

HOPE LIVES

The Lord lifts up those
who are bowed down

DAY 6: DOWNWARD MOBILITY

"The Lord lifts up those who are bowed down."
—PSALM 146:8

"Do not conform any longer to the pattern of this world, but be transformed by the renewing of your mind."
—ROMANS 12:2

I've realized that, more than I'd like to admit, I've been affected by what the world values—achievement, individualism, money, and busyness. I've allowed my heart to become cold when it encounters the needs of this world. And I want to change. I can be tempted to try to change myself…to close my eyes, scrunch up my nose, and think happy, compassionate thoughts—willing myself into the compassionate person I want to be. But I've tried that before, and I know it doesn't last.

What I need is God to transform me. I need the Holy Spirit to change me and the Scriptures to renew my mind so I won't "conform any longer to the pattern of this world."

Blessed Are the Poor

What I need is a complete reversal of perspective from the values the world has ingrained in me. Our world has always valued the upwardly mobile, the dynamic, rich, influential, and impressive. But Henri J. M. Nouwen calls the way of Christ "*downward* mobility." Christ didn't scramble to elevate his position in the world. Instead he willingly moved downward—far, far downward. And not only did he assume the lowest position, he placed special value on those around him who were also in the lowest positions. He said:

> **Blessed are the poor in spirit, for theirs is the kingdom of heaven.**
>
> **Blessed are those who mourn, for they will be comforted.**
>
> **Blessed are the meek, for they will inherit the earth.**
>
> **Blessed are those who hunger and thirst for righteousness, for they will be filled.**
>
> **—Matthew 5:3-6**

Growing up Christian, I've heard these verses so many times. "Blessed are the poor...blah, blah, blah." So I have to slow down and really take them in. God really does have a special care for the poor in spirit, the mourning, the meek, and those who hunger for justice. God knows how hardheaded I can be, so he brought these words alive to me on a visit to a home in Kenya.

Thabitha

I was with a group of Americans visiting a Compassion International Child Survival Program, a program that helps at-risk infants and toddlers around the world survive and thrive. We had the honor of being invited to visit Thabitha's home, the mother of one of the infants in the program. She lived in a two-acre slum. My aunt back home lives on two acres of land...but on these two acres in Africa, 4,000 people live. The path to Thabitha's home was a slippery mound of mud and trash. Stray chicks and tiny puppies nosed about in the mounds for food. We were suddenly hit by so many smells...sweat, mud, sewage, fire...as we passed the homes pieced together with corrugated metal, sticks, and garbage can lids.

When the children saw the troop of us coming, they started running, yelling, "Wazungu! Wazungu!" (White people! White people!) Many of them looked like they had been playing dress-up in some rich kid's toy box—one girl wore a torn purple satin party dress many sizes too large, another a pink dress that fell off one shoulder. Some children wanted nothing more than to give us a high five and sing out, "How are you?" We called back, "Jambo!" (which we later learned was "hello" in the *wrong* dialect). Other children looked despondently on from the edge of the road. One boy, about 6, watched us pass as he held his younger brother, whose arms and head fell listlessly to the side.

Thabitha had been trained by the Child Survival Program on how to start a small shoe-repair business in order to become self-sufficient. Before we visited her home, she proudly escorted us to her new shop. It was a tiny stand, pieced together from scraps of wood. She showed us where she would sit each day with her baby boy, Daniel, at her side while she sewed the soles onto shoes. Her eyes gleamed with joy and pride at her 4-foot-wide stand.

She then led us back to her home, through winding, up-and-down alleys like an obstacle course, dodging sewage ditches and ducking under laundry lines. Thabitha's home was tiny and dark, one low-ceilinged room. The only light came in through a patch of yellow plastic about 9 inches across, which begrudged a dull glow to enter the room, making it look like dusk at noon. As she sat smiling proudly at the guests stooped inside her home, she told us of her dreams: to get a window with the money she was making and for her boy to become a pastor. A small window to let light into her home and a son who loved God—those were her greatest desires.

In that cramped room, Thabitha's bright eyes shone with so much hope and so much gratitude they electrified the dark space. And in that moment, I was struck. A voice whispered, *This is it. This* is who God calls blessed. The poor and meek who thirst for justice—this is Thabitha. This single mother living in a dark home down a treacherous alley in a corner of Africa making money to feed her baby by sewing soles on

Thabitha

shoes—this is God's delight. And you could see it in her eyes. She knew she was a valued child of God. In that second, all my accomplishments (however few)—my degree, my title, my knowledge, my possessions—were nothing, absolutely nothing, in comparison with this woman. God's love filled that room, emanating out of *her*.

As I left, I told Thabitha, feeling humbled and awkward, that she was beautiful and I could see the light of Christ in her eyes. "Really?" she asked with delight, the delight of a humble woman who yet knows she is loved by God. This woman would be nothing in the estimation of nearly all society. But God allowed me to glimpse that she is *great* in the kingdom of heaven. *"Has not God chosen those who are poor in the eyes of the world to be rich in faith and to inherit the kingdom he promised those who love him?"* (James 2:5).

This woman's faith was thick—you could feel it in that room. Mine felt thin and stretched next to it.

A group of children had gathered outside, wanting a peek at the *wazungu*. And as we left the home, a local pastor who had joined us on the trip led the children, who clearly adored him, in a round of a hymn. He'd sing out, "Are you happy?" and the children, with muddy faces, torn dresses, standing on a trash mound, would shout back, "Yes, we're happy!" Those children, that pastor, that mother were rich in faith. And I, with my gleamingly clean apartment back home, 401(k), and stable job, wanted to be like them.

" 'Who is the greatest in the kingdom of heaven?' He called a little child and had him stand among them. And he said: 'I tell you the truth, unless you change and become like little children, you will never enter the kingdom of heaven. Therefore, whoever humbles himself like this child is the greatest in the kingdom of heaven.' "

—MATTHEW 18:1-4

Greatest in the Kingdom of Heaven

This verse seems to have been written directly to me: *"God chose things the world considers foolish in order to shame those who think they are wise. And he chose things that are powerless to shame those who are powerful. God chose things despised by the world, things counted as nothing at all, and used them to bring to nothing what the world considers important"* (1 Corinthians 1:27-28, NLT).

The humblest child is the greatest—that little girl in a torn and dirty party dress singing of her joy in God on a trash heap—she's the greatest in the kingdom of heaven. Those people our world tells us are nothing are great in God's reckoning. And they are the ones who can teach me.

It's not that God loves the poor any more than he loves me or anyone else in America—he's not a reverse social snob. He loves the wealthy deeply, as I can see in his interactions with the rich young man in Mark 10, the same man who prompted Jesus to say, "It is easier for a camel to go through the eye of a needle than for a rich man to enter the kingdom of God" (Mark 10:25). Despite this, "Jesus looked at [the rich young man] and loved him" (Mark 10:21).

I know Jesus looks at me—with *all* my struggles—and loves me. In his compassion he sees what is lacking in my faith and wants to heal my soul. He knows I need the humility and faith of the poor that I can so easily lose in my material abundance. I need to take spiritual lessons from the poor, learning their rich, childlike faith.

Downward mobility—becoming like and loving the poor—was at the heart of Christ's ministry: *"Who, being in very nature God, did not consider equality with God something to be grasped, but made himself nothing, taking the very nature of a servant, being made in human likeness. And being found in appearance as a man, he humbled himself and became obedient to death—even death on a cross!"* (Philippians 2:6-8). This is the attitude God asks of me—to live not for my own advancement, but for the good of others. When I become like the poor and like a child, God calls me blessed. I will have finally poked my head out of the smog of this world's backward values and peeked into his kingdom.

How can you allow God to transform your mind, to value what God values?

MY PRAYER

Dear Lord, I want to be like you. Please fill me with your Holy Spirit and use your Word to transform me. Help me to value what you value, to love those in this world who I've been conditioned to ignore. Help me to have faith that is rich and childlike, so I can see with your eyes.

DAY 7: OLD TESTAMENT JUSTICE

"He who oppresses the poor shows contempt for their Maker, but whoever is kind to the needy honors God."

—PROVERBS 14:31

As I read through the Old Testament looking for verses that relate to helping the poor, it's astounding how many are there. God truly is just and full of compassion and concern for those who could be overlooked or kept in the margins by society and set so many laws in place to ensure their provision. Widows, the fatherless, and orphans each have about 40 verses that command justice for them. The sheer volume of verses dedicated to those in the margins of society convinces me that their treatment is of *utmost importance* to God.

When reading the Old Testament prophets, it's easy to focus on how God condemned the Israelites because they were idolatrous. But that's only half the story; I find that in verse after verse, the prophets condemn the Israelites for their oppression of the poor. God did hate their idolatry, but he also considered their treatment of the poor, widows, and orphans cause to destroy their nation. God's condemnation of this treatment is found in many passages: "They refuse to defend the cause of orphans or fight for the rights of widows. Therefore, the Lord…says, 'I will take revenge on my enemies and pay back my foes! I will raise my fist against you' " (Isaiah 1:23-25, NLT). (See also Amos 2:6-7; 5:10-15; Ezekiel 16:49-50; Isaiah 10:1-3; 58; Jeremiah 5:26-29; 22:13-19.)

The law was given to the Israelites at a particular time in history, of course, and isn't directed at us. I am under the banner of grace—my salvation rests in Jesus' blood, not my good works. But I can glean from Old Testament law the kind of justice God wants to reign in society today. Old Testament justice is the backbone of Western civilization, one of the key influences in shaping the laws of America and the West. I can't help but be awed at the great tradition God set in place and by the compassionate and just God I serve.

Gleaning and Tithing

One law God set in place to ensure provision for the poor is tithing. "At the end of every three years, bring all the tithes of that year's produce and store it in your towns, so that the Levites (who have no allotment or inheritance of their own) and the aliens, the fatherless and the widows who live in your towns may come and eat and be satisfied" (Deuteronomy 14:28-29).

The law of gleaning is similar: "When you are harvesting in your field and you overlook a sheaf, do not go back to get it. Leave it for the alien, the fatherless and the widow, so that the Lord your God may bless you in all the work of your hands" (Deuteronomy 24:19). Those who owned no land or who had no other means of livelihood could still find provision. God's ideal of a righteous society is one that has provisions set in place for the alien, the widow, and the orphan, and these laws are the predecessors of modern welfare systems.

The law of gleaning was up to each individual landowner, and I wonder what that means for my life. I can "glean" from the law of tithing the types of social laws I would want to support in modern-day government and what I'd like my church tithe to support. But perhaps I can glean even more from the law of gleaning. Gleaning wasn't enforced by government; it was something landowners did individually to provide for others. It can be easy to rely on our government systems or church tithes to provide for the poor. But could this law of gleaning on top of tithing mean intentionally leaving aside a certain amount of my "crop" for those in need, even if my taxes and tithe are already supporting social welfare? I'm challenged to think that taking care of those in need isn't just a government or church concern, but also *my personal* concern.

The Sabbath Year and the Year of Jubilee

God also shows his desire that we provide out of our wealth for the poor in the Sabbath Year and the Year of Jubilee. In Exodus 23:10-11, God commands: "For six years you are to sow your fields and harvest the crops, but during the seventh year let the land lie unplowed and unused. Then the poor among your people may get food from it." In the Sabbath Year, Hebrew slaves were also to gain their freedom. "If a fellow Hebrew, a man or a woman, sells himself to you and serves you six years, in the seventh year you must let him go free. And when you release him, do not send him away empty-handed. Supply him liberally from your flock, your threshing floor and your winepress. Give to him as the Lord your God has blessed you" (Deuteronomy

15:12-14; see also Exodus 21:2-6). Not only were the Israelites to free their servants, they were to do it extravagantly.

The third provision of the Sabbath Year was to cancel all debt after the sixth year so that "there should be no poor among [them]" (Deuteronomy 15:4). The heart of the Sabbath Year was this: "If there is a poor man among [you]…do not be hardhearted or tightfisted toward your poor brother. Rather be openhanded and freely lend him whatever he needs…Give generously to him and do so without a grudging heart…Be openhanded toward your brothers and toward the poor and needy in your land" (Deuteronomy 15:7-11).

The Year of Jubilee came every 50 years, a year for all land to return to its ancestral owners, with the opportunity for the original "owners" to buy back the land at uninflated prices. This allowed for a relatively even distribution of wealth—one landowner would never grow too powerful while another had no way of providing for his family (Leviticus 25:8-55).

I see from these laws that occasional charity wasn't God's justice. The redistribution of land, freeing of servants, and cancellation of debt ensured economic opportunity for all Israelites. In these laws, I see that God values an equality among his people that allows each the basic necessities to be a thriving, contributing member of society.

How does this relate to me now? Again, it can guide me in the social laws I support and in key issues today such as debt relief in developing countries. It also reminds me of the spirit I should have in my giving. When I approach the issue of poverty, it's easy to feel solemn, but *jubilee* means "celebration." It's with a spirit of rejoicing that I want to approach serving the poor. God is an awesome and compassionate God, and he is worth celebrating! In giving to others, I'm celebrating my amazing God and sharing him with others.

It reminds me of something Jesus said: "When you give a luncheon or dinner, do not invite your friends, your brothers or relatives, or your rich neighbors; if you do, they may invite you back and so you will be repaid. But when you give a banquet, invite the poor, the crippled, the lame, the blind, and you will be blessed" (Luke 14:12-14). When I give to others, it can be a party—literally! Compassion isn't condescending to drop a few coins in a can; it's welcoming fellow humans into the celebration of God's abundance. Maybe I'll just have to throw a party…

The Oppression of Workers and Justice for the Poor

Besides the passages on specific social practices, the Old Testament repeatedly instructs the Israelites not to oppress their workers and to give the poor a fair trial. "Do not deny justice to your poor people in their lawsuits" (Exodus 23:6; see also Psalm 72:1-4 and Amos 5:10-15). "Lighten the burden of those who work for you. Let the oppressed go free, and remove the chains that bind people" (Isaiah 58:6, NLT). God's justice demands that those in power and with wealth treat the poor with the same dignity and justice as they do the wealthy.

What does oppression of workers have to do with me? Of course, I'd never oppress workers or not give them fair wages—I don't even employ anyone to oppress! But these verses can guide the purchasing choices I make. The following passage affects me deeply:

> The Lord enters into judgment against the elders and leaders of his people: "...The plunder from the poor is in your houses. What do you mean by crushing my people and grinding the faces of the poor?" declares the Lord, the Lord Almighty.
>
> The Lord says, "The women of Zion are haughty, walking along with outstretched necks, flirting with their eyes, tripping along with mincing steps, with ornaments jingling on their ankles. Therefore the Lord will bring sores on the heads of the women of Zion; the Lord will make their scalps bald." In that day the Lord will snatch away their finery: the bangles and headbands and crescent necklaces, the earrings and bracelets and veils...Instead of fragrance there will be a stench; instead of a sash, a rope; instead of well-dressed hair, baldness; instead of fine clothing, sackcloth; instead of beauty, branding.
>
> —Isaiah 3:14-24

God condemns those who "grind the face of the poor." In the next sentence, he condemns the women of Zion for their luxurious lifestyles, assumedly made possible by the oppression of the poor. It's very possible that the women of Zion knew little or nothing about the conditions of the workers who enabled their finery. They weren't in the fields. They were simply enjoying their wealth, probably without giving much thought to the workers—even if they knew just a little bit. But these women were condemned outright.

Is there a similarity between the haughty women of Zion and me—enjoying the luxuries my money buys? I don't think of myself as the lazy rich, lounging on a couch and being fed grapes by servants. But that's just because luxury is commonplace around here. One example is coffee. Coffee is a luxury (*not* a necessity, however much I feel it's imperative to my well-being) that I can afford to have imported. Too often, farmers who grow coffee in places such as South America aren't treated with justice—the wages industries pay for their goods keep them trapped in poverty, not being enough to feed their families, send their children to school, or thrive. (You *can* buy coffee and other products such as chocolate, bananas, and tea with a fair trade guarantee at many stores such as Trader Joe's, Whole Foods, and Starbucks.)

This isn't a simple right or wrong issue—these industries are sometimes the only thing keeping some farmers from death. But I do have to question whether God implicates me in the oppression of workers when I purposely buy cheaper products from companies I know are exploiting the poor rather than buying those goods from companies that ensure fair payment of workers. The passage in Isaiah convinces me that God has a high standard for the choices I make, and I need to buy with my eyes open wide.

What one passage challenged you the most? Is there an action or change you feel convicted to make based on this Scripture?

MY PRAYER

Dear God, I praise you for the order you set forth in this world. You are just and compassionate. Thank you for the Scriptures that teach me how to live and how to treat others. Please show me from these Scriptures how you want me to live my life. If there is an area that you would change, please convict me that I might become more like Christ. I want to have the same concern for those in the margins of society that you have. Please transform me though contemplating your Word.

DAY 8: BECOMING LIKE CHRIST

"Freely you have received, freely give."
—MATTHEW 10:8

I've seen what the Old Testament has to say about helping those in need. So what can I learn from the New Testament, from Jesus?

Compassion vs. Savior Complex

The most notable thing about Jesus in regard to the poor isn't necessarily what he said. It's what he did. He had only a handful of years of ministry, and he chose to spend a large amount of that time in relative obscurity helping people in need. That was of utmost importance to him. It's not exactly what I'd expect of a great teacher today—I'd expect him to invest his time for maximum impact. Hit the key influential leaders and be seen by the most people.

But Jesus chose to spend much of his time in a way that, according to these standards, would seem to have little lasting impact. Some blind guy in the middle of nowhere got his sight back. He most likely didn't go on to start any great church movements. He probably went on to live a quiet life. It wouldn't seem that this act would have much lasting influence or positive repercussions on the world. Yet Jesus spent much of his time healing individuals, one at a time, in obscurity.

Individuals matter to God. Jesus' healing of the blind man had lasting, positive effects on that one man, his soul, and probably the souls of his family, neighbors, and descendants. That was enough to merit Jesus' precious time. Sometimes I hesitate to serve, thinking, "What difference will it make? Nothing ever changes; poverty will never end." In that thought, I am unlike Jesus. It makes a difference to one person, and even if all the good that comes of my service stops right there (which is unlikely), that is enough. It was enough for Jesus. He, the God of the universe, was content to touch one person's life.

I can be a serving megalomaniac—striving for only grand changes. I have a savior complex, and since I fear my efforts won't end in grandiosity, I'm tempted not to try at all. That's pride. Jesus could have had a savior complex if anyone could, but he was humble enough to stop and heal one obscure man. Jesus was motivated by compassion: "When he saw the crowds, he had compassion on them, because they were harassed and helpless, like sheep without a shepherd" (Matthew 9:36). "When Jesus landed and saw a large crowd, he had compassion on them and healed their sick" (Matthew 14:14). When Jesus looked at this world, he wasn't thinking about influence, he was responding in compassion. I want my motivation to be compassion and love, not a desire to do something big.

Freely Give

Jesus says, "Freely you have received, freely give" (Matthew 10:8). I've received a lot from Christ, and all of it has been free to me. That's the measure to use when showing compassion. Jesus also says, "Give to the one who asks you, and do not turn away from the one who wants to borrow from you" (Matthew 5:42), even giving up our coat, too, if sued in court for our shirt (Matthew 5:40). I'm to give above even what is asked of me. True Christ-like generosity goes beyond just requirement. And giving isn't just about money. Jesus didn't have wealth to give when he walked this earth. What he gave was attention, dignity, love, and respect to people as individual images of God. When I treat people like that, I'm giving them the greatest gift I have to give.

Jesus holds nothing back from me. He forgave me abundantly, he loves me abundantly, and he gives to me abundantly. That same spirit is what I want to have toward others. When asked what was most important, Jesus said first to love God and second to love your neighbor as yourself. The most important thing, second to loving God, is to love people. And not just any love, but over-the-top generous, self-sacrificing love. That's what I'm called to freely give to others.

The Scary Speech

Jesus gave one oration regarding helping the poor. But it's not a fun one.

When the Son of Man comes in his glory...All the nations will be gathered before him, and he will separate the people one from another as a shepherd separates the sheep from the goats...

Then the King will say to those on his right, "Come, you who are blessed by my Father; take your inheritance...For I was hungry and you gave me something to eat, I was thirsty and you gave me something to drink, I was a stranger and you invited me in, I needed clothes and you clothed me, I was sick and you looked after me, I was in prison and you came to visit me."

Then the righteous will answer him, "Lord, when did we see you hungry and feed you, or thirsty and give you something to drink?"...

The King will reply, "I tell you the truth, whatever you did for one of the least of these brothers of mine, you did for me." Then he will say to those on his left, "Depart from me, you who are cursed, into the eternal fire prepared for the devil and his angels. For I was hungry and you gave me nothing to eat, I was thirsty and you gave me nothing to drink, I was a stranger and you did not invite me in, I needed clothes and you did not clothe me, I was sick and in prison and you did not look after me."

They also will answer, "Lord, when did we see you hungry or thirsty or a stranger or needing clothes or sick or in prison, and did not help you?"

He will reply, "I tell you the truth, whatever you did not do for one of the least of these, you did not do for me." Then they will go away to eternal punishment, but the righteous to eternal life.

—Matthew 25:31-46

According to this passage, if I see someone hungry and I don't feed him, if I see someone naked and don't clothe him...I'm going to hell. Now wait a minute! The epistles teach that salvation is through faith by grace alone and not by good works. How does Matthew 25:31-46 fit into "salvation through grace alone"?

First John 3:17 helps me understand: "If anyone has material possessions and sees his brother in need but has no pity on him, how can the love of God be in him?" Can God's love be in me if I don't help those in need? John isn't asking lightly—in this passage, he's referring to heaven and hell. He reasons that, "We know that we have passed from death to life, because we love our brothers. Anyone who does not love remains in death" (verse 14)—that is, spiritually dead. In the next several verses, John says "let us not love with words or tongue but with actions and in truth. This then is how we know that we belong to the truth, and how we set our hearts at rest in his presence" (verses 18-19). John isn't saying that helping or loving others gains us salvation. But he is questioning how we can be Christ's followers if we *do not* help others. If I have no *actions* of helping a brother in need, my heart can't be "at rest" when I stand before God.

This is heavy. Am I Christ's follower if I don't help others? There have been times I have hardened my heart to the needs of others. These verses make serious and strong claims that can't be ignored. The truth is that if I follow Christ, I will act like Christ. And if I'm not acting like Christ, I need to evaluate the sincerity of my faith.

Philippians 2:12-13 encourages me: "Continue to work out your salvation with fear and trembling, for it is God who works in you to will and to act according to his good purpose." This isn't all up to me. God is working in me, to change me and give me his love of others. I'm not perfect. I have made and will continue to make mistakes. But God is the one at work in me, as I continue to work out my salvation, and he will bless my desire to become more like Christ.

Helping those in need is central to following Christ. It is who he is, and therefore, who I am. To know God is irrevocably woven into loving others, and I'll never know God in his fullness without extending that kind of love. I know a man who is dedicated to serving the poor. I asked him why he does it, and he said, "Serving the poor, I grow closer to God and see Jesus more clearly. It helps me see Jesus because I'm doing what he would be doing if he were there. I go about life in pretty routine ways—get up, eat, go to work—and think about Jesus from time to time. But when I'm working with the poor, Jesus is front and center in my mind. It's like I sense him to be more real and more close during those times. It slows you down. It catches you and makes you think about why you're doing what you're doing."

Jeremiah states it well: " 'He defended the cause of the poor and needy, and so all went well. Is that not what it means to know me?' declares the Lord" (Jeremiah 22:16).

We know God when we help and love others. We become Christ to those we help, a manifestation of his love. One of the great mysteries God has placed in this universe is that when I do good to others, I'm doing it to Christ, too. Wess Stafford, the president of Compassion International, tells a story that captures this mystery perfectly, understood by the eyes of a child.

"Mister, are you Jesus?" The question from the little Haitian lad I had met on the grimy streets of Port-au-Prince startled me. The sincerity in his dark eyes cautioned me to not take his inquiry lightly. What on earth could have prompted the question?

My mind retraced my steps since I had met little Jean Pierre that morning. He had been sitting on the curb outside the local KFC, where the restaurant's exhaust vent blasted the smell of fried chicken to mingle with the usual stench of rotting garbage that filled the streets. Jean Pierre was eating a crust of bread as I walked by. Our eyes met, and I paused to talk with him. He explained that "if you eat a crust of bread beneath these vents, it makes it taste like chicken." We shared a laugh, and I walked on. Jean Pierre followed me at a distance. I forgot about him and went about my business.

At Madam Sarah's corner, I bought a handful of peanuts for 20 cents. I thanked her and walked off before she could finish digging in her basket for change. I gave the nuts to a man begging at the next corner. I got my shoes shined four or five times. Not that they needed it, but it gave me a few precious moments with a child or an old man who needed a kind word and the few cents for their work. My car likewise was washed numerous times each day with the filthy water that ran down the street gutters. Each occasion gave me the excuse to joke with the child who graced me with his industriousness. A generous tip, a hug, exaggerated admiration at the splendor of my "shiny" car, and a word about his being the very best car washer in all of the city, and I pressed on.

Jean Pierre had clandestinely taken all of this in and had come to the conclusion that a man who did these sorts of things must, in fact, be Jesus! What a mistake! What an honor! What an opportunity.

Adapted from a story by Wess Stafford.

When I take a simple step to love and lend dignity to a creation of God, I am truly becoming Christ to that person…and glimpsing who Christ truly is. And God has given rich faith to the pure eyes of a child to be able to see him.

If you look at your current actions of love toward others, what conclusion do you draw about your faith in light of the passage you read in 1 John?

MY PRAYER

Dear Lord, I praise you that you are a God of compassion. I thank you that you value the fate of each individual. Please help me to become more like you. I want to have your love and compassion for the people I encounter. Please work in me and change me to be more like you.

DAY 9: NEW TESTAMENT COMMUNITY

"A generous man will prosper; he who refreshes others will himself be refreshed."

—PROVERBS 11:25

I've soaked in what the Old Testament has to say about the poor and have examined Jesus' actions among the poor, and so I want to know: How did the early church live—with all the knowledge of the Old Testament and all the immediacy of Jesus' actions? I'm not disappointed by what I find. When I read of their actions toward one another, I'm reminded of new Christians I've known. I remember college days when several freshmen I knew became Christians. They had such fire and zeal. With bright eyes, they wanted to do crazy things for God. They wanted to live radically different lives of deep commitment to Christ and to one another. If anyone would sell their possessions and live in communion with one another, they would be the ones.

"All the believers . . . shared everything they had. They sold their property and possessions and shared the money with those in need. They...shared their meals with great joy and generosity— all the while praising God and enjoying the goodwill of all the people."

—ACTS 2:44-47, NLT

> "All the believers were united in heart and mind. And they felt that what they owned was not their own, so they shared everything they had . . . There were no needy people among them, because those who owned land or houses would sell them and bring the money to the apostles to give to those in need."
>
> —ACTS 4:32-35, NLT

These early followers of Christ had that new-believer zeal. They were willing to do crazy things, like selling their homes, in order to help others. Their excitement is palpable. I read this, and I feel old and jaded. When you've just begun to follow Christ, anything seems possible, nothing is out of bounds. It's an exciting new adventure with your new family, the church. I look smilingly, condescendingly on. *How cute. Another zealous baby Christian. Isn't that sweet? It won't last long.*

Because something happens when you've been following Christ for a while. Selling your own home starts to sound a little, well, young and naïve. Living that radical life of the early church seems like a great ideal to use as a base for a sermon...but not something I'd *actually* do. It's just so extreme. I hear these crazy, radical things the early church did and want all or nothing—to do something big and grand...or to just not bother at all. I don't really feel compelled to sell my possessions, and so I dismiss the community of the early church as a zealous and unrealistic anomaly.

Once again, my motivation for helping others can never be guilt or a sense of obligation or a savior complex. These motives either won't be enough to get me over the hump of inaction or will fizzle out. And it's comforting to see that the early church's generosity wasn't prompted by a legalistic standard. When Ananias sold his property and gave some of the money to the church, Peter said, "The property was yours to sell or not sell, as you wished. And after selling it, the money was also yours to give away" (Acts 5:4, NLT). The early Christians sold their possessions as they felt compelled by the Holy Spirit, not by obligation or by guilt.

Members of the early church weren't only compelled to sell their homes. Aristides, a Christian philosopher, wrote regarding the church: "If there is among them a man that is poor and needy, and they have not an abundance of necessaries, they fast two or three days that they may supply the needy with their necessary food." God compelled some to give houses; God compelled others to give up food. When we're filled with the love of Christ, God will compel us each in a different way. The essential for me is to seek God, asking that I'll be filled with his love for the church. Then, I can ask him what exactly he wants me to do.

I have a friend, Mark, who did just this. It started with a mission trip to Juarez with his family. They visited a barrio of 20,000 that sat on the edge of the city dump. And he was floored. He saw people living in conditions he'd never seen, conditions he couldn't even comprehend. There was no sanitation, no water; there were no roads. The smell alone was indescribable, and thousands lived in shelters pieced together from pieces scavenged from the dump. It was, as he put it, "a big face full." After seeing the conditions and interacting with the people in the church they were visiting, he just couldn't reconcile his experiences. He couldn't understand how this could happen, why there was no help for them.

He and his family went home. That first night home, Mark passed his 8-year-old daughter's room and saw her sitting on her bed staring at the wall. She had a beautiful room, the walls lined with teddy bears and dolls. He asked her why she wasn't in bed, and she looked at him with tears in her eyes and said, "Dad, I just have way too much. How come I have so much when others have so little?"

It was at that point that Mark and his family began to pray, asking God what he wanted them to do to help others. They began to understand that God's plan entailed so much more than they were involved in. God began to reveal that "we are blessed to be a blessing." Eventually that translated into many areas of their lives including trading their 3,200-square-foot home with two dining rooms and two living rooms for a 1,500-square-foot home, cutting their mortgage to a third of what it was. They did it so they could live more simply and be more generous. And, although it wasn't their intention, it has drawn his family closer together and made them all more comfortable.

So I guess I'm the naïve one—there are still people devoted enough to sell their homes. And I find encouragement in the Apostle Paul's words: "Here is my advice… Give in proportion to what you have. Whatever you give is acceptable if you give it eagerly. And give according to what you have, not what you don't have. Of course, I don't mean your giving should make life easy for others and hard for yourselves. I only mean that there should be some equality. Right now you have plenty and can help those who are in need. Later, they will have plenty and can share with you when you need it" (2 Corinthians 8:10-14, NLT). Earlier in the same passage he says, "I am not commanding you to do this. But I am testing how genuine your love is…You know the generous grace of our Lord Jesus Christ. Though he was rich, yet for your sakes he became poor, so that by his poverty he could make you rich" (2 Corinthians 8:8-9, NLT). Gifts can't be commanded or required; they are given out of love and grace. We give freely and eagerly because Christ first gave to us.

And it's not all about money. God created the parts of the body of Christ to serve different roles, to help those in need in different ways. Money isn't the only way I can help. I don't have a house to give, but I can make a mean enchilada casserole. Some have the gift of giving, some the gift of prayer, some the gift of hospitality, others the gift of encouragement. There's no spiritual hierarchy as to which is more righteous— it's not inherently better to give a house than a meal; it's not inherently better to share hospitality than to encourage. It's all about what God is asking of *me*.

Who Is My Neighbor? Local vs. Global

Who exactly does God want me to help? There are plenty of poor in America, in churches around here. Does God call me to help those abroad, too? The early church's example is pretty clear: They all gave in common so that the church everywhere would have enough. They gave across racial and geographic lines—from Europe to Asia and from Gentiles to Jews. Here's the eagerness with which they desired to help:

"Now I want you to know, dear brothers and sisters, what God in his kindness has done through the churches in Macedonia. They are being tested by many troubles, and they are very poor. But they are also filled with abundant joy, which has overflowed in rich generosity. For I can testify that they gave not only what they could afford, but far more. And they did it of their own free will. They begged us again and again for the privilege of sharing in the gift for the believers in Jerusalem. They even did more than we had hoped, for their first action was to give themselves to the Lord and to us."

—2 CORINTHIANS 8:1-5, NLT

These Macedonians' joy was so great that even though they were poor, they *begged* to give to those in need on another continent. The genesis of their generosity was their devotion to Christ—their first action was to give themselves to the Lord, which resulted in generosity above what Paul had hoped for. This doesn't mean I'm commanded to give to churches abroad. But it does show that when I devote myself first to the Lord, he may inspire me to. He'll inspire some to give to the members of their own church, and he'll inspire some churches to give to the church next door or the church in Asia.

But besides giving to the church, what about giving to those in need locally as well as globally, Christian as well as non-Christian? An expert in the law wanting to know how to inherit eternal life asked Jesus what he ought to do. Jesus told him to do what the Law says: " 'Love the Lord your God with all your heart, all your soul, all your strength, and all your mind.' And, 'Love your neighbor as yourself.' " The man, trying to find a loophole, asked, "And who is my neighbor?" This launched Jesus into the parable of the good Samaritan (Luke 10:25-37, NLT). He told of a Jewish man who was attacked and left lying on the side of the road. Two Jewish passersby didn't stop to help, but the Samaritan, a man from a despised neighboring race, stopped and helped the man. Jesus concluded, "Go and do the same."

The neighbor I am called to love isn't only someone from the same race, the same town, or the same church. My neighbor is whoever is in need, whoever God has placed in my path. God hasn't, obviously, asked each individual to help everyone everywhere in need. The church throughout the world in concert will tend to the needs of this world. And it seems that God shows us what good works he has for us through our experiences and our hearts. He put the woman in Amsterdam in my path, which has given me a heart to help women and children who are being trafficked in the sex business. He put a friend of mine in the path of inner-city kids in Los Angeles, which fired her passion to mentor underprivileged children. "For we are God's workmanship, created in Christ Jesus to do good works, which God prepared in advance for us to do" (Ephesians 2:10).

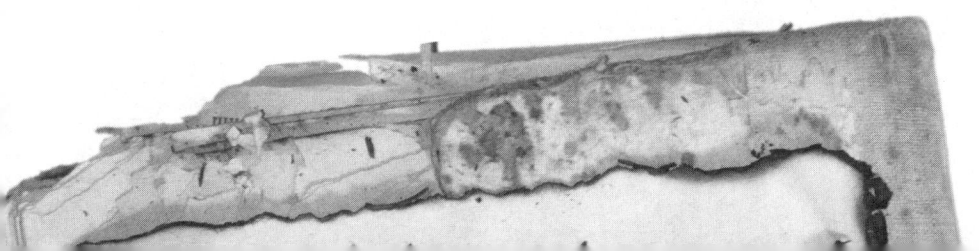

Read 2 Corinthians 8. Write about your love for the church, whether it's hot or cold, and how you think God has created you to serve the body of Christ.

DAY 10: THE PURSUIT OF HAPPINESS

"True godliness with contentment is itself great wealth."
—1 TIMOTHY 6:6, NLT

"Therefore I tell you, do not worry about your life, what you will eat or drink; or about your body, what you will wear. Is not life more important than food, and the body more important than clothes?...But seek first his kingdom and his righteousness, and all these things will be given to you as well."
—MATTHEW 6:25-33

I've read so many verses that reveal God's desire for me to value what he values and to help those around me. How, then, should I live? How can I love what God treasures instead of pursuing what the world treasures? I hate to harp about money, but honestly, the Bible *does* harp about money when it comes to helping others. Where my heart is on this particular issue will expose where my heart is in regard to the poor—and once God has straightened out this key issue in my heart, my openness and love for the poor will be able to overflow.

I was watching *Good Morning America* the other day and saw a news story that revealed one of the lies of American culture. Amid chuckles from the anchors, one anchor asked his interviewee, "Dee, can you honestly say that you're *actually* happy?" Dee used to live in a large home, but after visiting Guatemala, she decided to "smart-size" her home and moved into an 84-square-foot home—very similar to the size of homes lived in by countless families elsewhere in the world. Her response to the anchor: "Yes, I love it!" She loves the extra time and money she has to give to others and a simple, less complicated life. The anchors of the show couldn't help but glance at one another and laugh uncomfortably. Their incredulity was clear. They just couldn't quite believe that someone could live like that and be happy.

I find myself operating with an underlying motivator I'm not necessarily even conscious of—the motivator of upward mobility—doing what I'm doing so I can get to that next level of American achievement: job title, then car, then home, then kids, then promotion, and on and on. Subconsciously, I've come to believe that in order to be happy, I need to keep up with the status quo and keep moving up. But is that true? It wasn't true for Dee or my friend Mark—they gave up the status quo and found contentment instead in generosity. They live this verse: "Do not store up for yourselves treasures on earth, where moth and rust destroy, and where thieves break in and steal. But store up for yourselves treasures in heaven, where moth and rust do not destroy, and where thieves do not break in and steal" (Matthew 6:19-20). Instead of storing up temporal goods, they invested in treasures that are eternal.

We could probably all tell stories of people we know who heedlessly sought money for money's sake. The stories I could tell are all sad stories—they include bitterness and jealousy and broken families and disappointment. Wealth for wealth's sake only brings destruction. "People who want to get rich fall into temptation and a trap and into many foolish and harmful desires that plunge men into ruin and destruction. For the love of money is a root of all kinds of evil. Some people, eager for money, have wandered from the faith and pierced themselves with many griefs" (1 Timothy 6:9-10).

Rather than senseless "moving on up," the Bible prescribes this: "We brought nothing into the world, and we can take nothing out of it. But if we have food and clothing, we will be content with that" (1 Timothy 6:7-8). And: "Do not wear yourself out to get rich; have the wisdom to show restraint" (Proverbs 23:4).

Use Your Wealth

The *love* of money is evil, but money itself isn't. Many of us are already wealthy. How, then, should we live? "Command those who are rich in this present world not to be arrogant nor to put their hope in wealth, which is so uncertain, but to put their hope in God, who richly provides us with everything for our enjoyment. Command them to do good, to be rich in good deeds, and to be generous and willing to share" (1 Timothy 6:17-18).

God has given me wealth so that I can be rich in good works, generous, and willing to share. I've been entrusted with an investment. My in-laws are particularly good at this. My mother-in-law was raised with all the wealth she could have wanted and knows that it, in itself, doesn't bring happiness. My father-in-law is a doctor and over the years has earned quite enough to live very well. But instead of using their wealth only to live extravagantly, they use their wealth as a means to bless others. Their real joy is in giving to others.

Seeing how they live reminds me that enjoying wealth isn't wrong—God "richly provides us with everything *for our enjoyment.*" God created the good things in this world, in part, just to bring us pleasure and joy! And we truly experience this pleasure when we openhandedly enjoy God's creation and all the good in it *with others.* Relationship is central to Christianity—the most important commandment is to love God, and the second is to love your neighbor. I think this applies to wealth. I'm to accept it as a loving gift from my Father, and I'm to enjoy it in relationship with other people. It's all about relationships; it's nothing to do with money. Again, my in-laws are great at this. Besides being generous to those in need, they use their wealth to build relationships, to share love. It's their greatest joy to give gifts to their children and their grandchildren. They love to use their wealth to bring their family together on vacations, in experiences, and (much to my delight) to spend long evenings with my husband and me at nice restaurants, lingering over good food and good conversation to build our relationships.

True Riches

In all of these passages of Scripture, I see hints of something more. If it's not riches that are the ultimate good in life, it's something better. Jesus gives hints of what the true good is. Rather than storing up wealth on earth, he tells us to store up "treasures in heaven" (Matthew 6:20). First Timothy also gives a hint of what these treasures are: "Command them to do good, to be rich in good deeds, and to be generous and willing to share. *In this way they will lay up treasure for themselves* as a firm foundation for the coming age, so that they may take hold of the life that is truly life" (1 Timothy 6:18-19).

What are the true treasures? The Bible never states explicitly, but I suspect that, in part, it's people. The treasures of this earth are temporal. The only thing on this earth that's eternal is people—the only treasure that doesn't end when this world does. Jesus makes the connection between giving to the poor and treasures in heaven: "Sell everything you have and give to the poor, and you will have treasure in heaven" (Luke 18:22). When we use wealth to help others, we're investing in an eternal treasure—a loved creation of God.

One of the great harms of poverty isn't physical, it's eternal, for it teaches souls who have never known Christ's love that they don't matter. Without the truth of Christ, a young boy's belief that he's a spectacular creation that matters to God and to this world can be crushed by poverty. And when those in poverty believe this lie and give up, these treasures of God are lost. What an honor that God has enabled us, in our own small ways, to show these people that they matter. That God has good for them. That they are loved.

Harriet is one of the precious treasures of God who nearly gave in to the lies of poverty. Born in a poor suburb of Kampala, Uganda, she faced huge obstacles. One of seven children, she never had anything of her own and would rotate clothing with her three sisters. Although Harriet was bright, at school she was singled out for her poverty rather than being praised for her work. "My most painful memory is when one of my classmates said my family must be really poor since my dad had only one pair of trousers. *I thought I did not matter at all to anyone.* I decided then to never speak up in class, and I began to dread going to school." It was a small occurrence, but for a young girl in a world where a lack of wealth defined her life as inconsequential, it devastated her sense of self-worth. The shame of poverty eclipsed her fragile self-esteem.

God wanted more for Harriet. Harriet's life was changed when she enrolled in a Compassion-assisted project, and a family abroad sponsored her. "I got photos from my sponsor, and I was very excited," Harriet says. "I thought at least it's someone…even if

Harriet

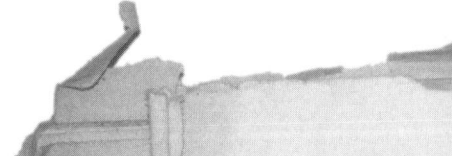

it's not someone that stays near me or someone that is in my class or in my school or in my community or in my country, *there's someone out there who loves me.*"

They weren't present, they didn't even live within 100 miles of her home, but the love of Harriet's sponsors began to fight the worst lie of poverty—that she didn't matter. And with that small spark of confidence, she was able to take her first steps. The project paid for her school fees, and Harriet began to forget her shame at school and started to blossom academically.

When examination time came, though, she didn't score high enough on her state exams to get a government scholarship to a university. The news was a serious blow to her still-fragile sense of self-worth. "I had lots of thoughts run through my mind," she says, "like becoming a prostitute since I had become a failure in life." Once again, the lies of poverty—that she was a failure, that she was nothing, that there was no hope for her—were whispering to Harriet that she might as well prostitute herself because she didn't matter. But God's love and the support from the project and her sponsors sustained Harriet. After graduating from high school, Harriet was accepted into Compassion's Leadership Development Program, which allowed her to obtain a university education.

Today, Harriet is a lawyer with the Uganda Human Rights Commission. She defied the lies of poverty and now works to help change the culture of violence permeating the poor and vulnerable in her country. Harriet's sponsors, by a simple act of faith and love, whispered God's truth into her ear. That small investment has multiplied. Harriet, this treasure of God, is now investing in the vulnerable children of Uganda, sharing God's love with the next generation. She has become a sponsor herself—she supports a boy named Bryan in Ecuador. What someone did for her, she wants to do for someone else.

I don't want to invest in wealth that doesn't last. I want to invest in an eternal treasure that will make me rich in God's eyes. I am honored by God to play this small role in his creation.

Spend time reflecting on what you treasure.
Confess what you have mistakenly treasured, and
write what you'd like to treasure.

MY PRAYER

Dear Lord, I praise you for your love of this world and for your plan for it. Thank you for taking me on this journey to restore my soul, to be more like you. Help me to turn away from the treasures of this world, which are only temporary and will rust. Please help me to treasure what is eternal and to use what you've given me to bless my relationships and to be generous and rich in good deeds.

Week Two
Reflection Questions

What was the most challenging truth you struggled through this week?

What can you do each day to ensure that you're viewing the people in this world through Christ's eyes?

Learning about the social justice the Old Testament prescribes, do you see any injustice around you that you think God is calling you to speak out against?

Is there someone in your life to whom you feel God calling you to be Christ?

Action Steps

1. Take some time to reread the verses covered in this week's readings. Open your Bible, and find all of the passages referenced this week. Ask God to use his Word to transform your mind.

2. Practice downward mobility. Visit a senior home, a hospital, or a homeless shelter, and spend time just talking to these people that God calls blessed. Look into their eyes, and ask God what you can learn from them.

3. Visit www.transfairusa.org to learn more about fair trade. Visit www.data.org to learn more about debt relief.

4. Look up the verses listed in Day 7 regarding laws of gleaning and tithing in the Old Testament. Take a look at your own finances, and (if you haven't already) consider how to implement a tithe (or more!) into your regular budget.

5. Speaking of investments…micro loans (starting at $50) are one way many Christians reach out to help those who need an opportunity to begin an income-generating activity. To learn more about micro loans, visit www.opportunity.org.

6. Visit www.persecution.com, the Web site for Voice of the Martyrs, to find out about the needs of the church worldwide. If you feel compelled, sign up for the free newsletter so you'll know how to pray for the church abroad.

Understanding
POVERTY

UNDERSTANDING POVERTY will guide the steps we take in releasing

others from it. This week we'll explore what poverty is—its causes and effects

and how it's a spiritual matter at its core.

hen I heard the voice
of the Lord saying,
Whom shall I send?

HOPE LIVES

And who will go for us?
And I said, Here am I.
Send me!

DAY 11: FOR SUCH A TIME AS THIS

"Then I heard the voice of the Lord saying,
'Whom shall I send? And who will go for us?'
And I said, 'Here am I. Send me!'"

—ISAIAH 6:8

Olive

Olive is a beautiful woman, with skin like dark coffee and eyes that flash. She is my age, born in the same year, and for some reason this makes me feel a strong connection—as a kid I might have played Hide and Seek in the street with her or sat next to her in math. Olive speaks of her life growing up in Uganda. I've heard statistics of poverty before, but those were faceless—they didn't have Olive's eyes or her white smile. The statistics are like annoying pebbles the news pelts me with. They fall to the ground and are forgotten.

Olive is different. She isn't one of the annoying numbers I'm bombarded with. She speaks of her life when she was 6. I think to myself, *What was I doing at 6?* First day of kindergarten with my new pink backpack and Mary Jane shoes. Pictures were taken, friends were made, cookies were gobbled. Your basic *Leave It to Beaver* episode. But at the same time I posed for pictures in my Mary Janes, rebels were spilling over Uganda's borders. Olive and her family lived in a small village. Someone ran, yelling that the rebels were coming. It was every man for himself. All dashed to the bushes and hid. The rebels swept through the village, killing those they found and burning huts on the way. Fleeing danger then became a regular occurrence for Olive. From the age of 6 to the age of 8, while I was eating Cheerios and watching *Sesame Street,* she was crouching in bushes, hoping not to be found and killed or, perhaps worse, forced to become a soldier's bride.

Next scene: 13 years old. I hated 13—I didn't make friends easily, and I was made fun of at school because my parents had bought me a *leather* skirt instead of a *suede* skirt, which was a must-have. But I was loved and safe and fed, embarrassing leather skirt and all. At 13, Olive had moved to the city with her mother where unrest wasn't knocking on the door each night. But Olive's mother had become ill. She was weak and getting weaker. One day Olive came home to bring her mother oranges. She was sleeping. Olive shook her. She didn't stir. Olive shook and shook, but her mom never woke up. Olive was an AIDS orphan at 13. Fifteen years later, telling the story, she holds her head in her hands as tears drip from her chin and her shoulders shake. This is no statistic; this is a daughter, just like me. This isn't a number that fell to the ground and was forgotten; this is 15 years of pain. This is a daughter who lost her mother too soon…while I was wishing my mom understood fashion trends better.

Without parents, Olive moved to a little house with seven of her cousins—all of whom had been orphaned. They slept stacked in different rooms. Olive slept in the kitchen with her sister. They scrounged for food. They took care of each other. They got by. The end of Olive's story is a happy one. Through a relief and development program, she had enough food to eat. She had enough money to pay for school fees. She got treatment when she had tuberculosis. She learned about the love of God and that he has a plan for her. And now she is a proud, tall woman with a master's degree in social work, helping children with disabilities. She isn't a number. She's a story of hope. She's a daughter. She's a friend. She's a treasure of God.

I'm Convinced

The pesky facts of poverty can bounce off of me. It's all so far away, the numbers are so big that they are just too much to digest (how many is a billion anyway?), and it's so much easier to just close my mind and move on. But then I think of Olive…and I'm convinced. I can't stand passively by anymore. That could have been *me*. That could have been *my* sister, who has her same flashing eyes. I can scarcely comprehend a life in which my sister and I would have to regularly run from men who are trying to kill us. But at 6, that could have been us; instead, it was Olive. At 13, it could have been me shaking my mother who never woke up. It was Olive. It could have been my cousins— Sarah, Katie, Greg, Tim, Tara, Chris, Kim—living with nothing and with no one to care for us. It was Olive and her cousins. I told my mom this story, and she trembled. It could have been her baby, her sweet little 6-year-old with a pink backpack and Mary Janes.

I'm convinced because those in poverty, the Olives, are just like me. I saw her. I looked into her eyes. A thin, thin line separates me from her. I'm convinced because I know God loves those I'd kind of like to forget. I've read the verses. I know the poor have a special place in God's heart. I know Jesus is somehow close to them, in them. I know that he wants me to free the oppressed, feed the hungry, and clothe the naked.

"God is in the slums, in the cardboard boxes
where the poor play house.
God is in the silence of a mother who
has infected her child with a virus that
will end both their lives. God is in
the cries heard under the rubble
of war. God is in the debris of wasted
opportunity and lives, and God is
with us if we are with them."

—BONO, LEAD SINGER OF U2

OK, God. I'm convinced…What do you want from me?

Such a Time

I could have just as easily been born in Uganda, running from rebels as a tot. But God chose differently. God "determined the times set for [men] and the exact places where they should live. God did this so that men would seek him and perhaps reach out for him and find him, though he is not far from each one of us" (Acts 17:26-27). God had a reason for placing me *exactly* when and where he did, as the daughter of a middle-class chiropractor in Aurora, Colorado. It might seem pretty random, but it was not.

Not only that, God also prepared particular good works for me: "We are God's workmanship, created in Christ Jesus to do good works, which God prepared in advance for us to do" (Ephesians 2:10). God has been planning and planning…placing me just so, giving me exactly what he has, that I might find him and that I might do the good he has prepared in advance for me. What exactly that is, I'm not sure yet. But I'm convinced there's something.

I think of Esther in the Bible. She was beautiful and charming and became a queen because of those qualities. She might have lain back, eaten grapes, and gotten shoulder rubs every day. I'd like that. But Esther chose to believe her uncle when he said, "Who knows but that you have come to royal position for such a time as this?" (Esther 4:14). "Such a time as this." Esther's husband, King Xerxes, had ordered a genocide of the Jews. Esther could have chosen to shut out the troubles of the world, stay quietly at home, and enjoy her very pleasant life. Instead, she used her position of power to speak up for the oppressed, risking not only her comfort, but her own life.

Could it be that God has placed me in a position of comfort and material power for such a time as this? A lack of clean water is killing almost 2 million people a year, 15.2 million children have lost one or both parents to AIDS, 1 billion people live in extreme poverty, and 1 million children are trafficked into exploitive labor each year. If ever there was "such a time"—a time that needs God's redemption, healing, and love—this is it.

I'm definitely not a savior of the world. Esther 4:14 says, "If you remain silent at this time, relief and deliverance…will arise from another place." That's a relief—because it's not about me. It seems God is on the move, always on the move, ready to raise up relief and deliverance, people who will go for him, who will be his hands. And maybe, just maybe, I am a part of that plan. Maybe God has given me what he has and put me where he has for just such a time as this.

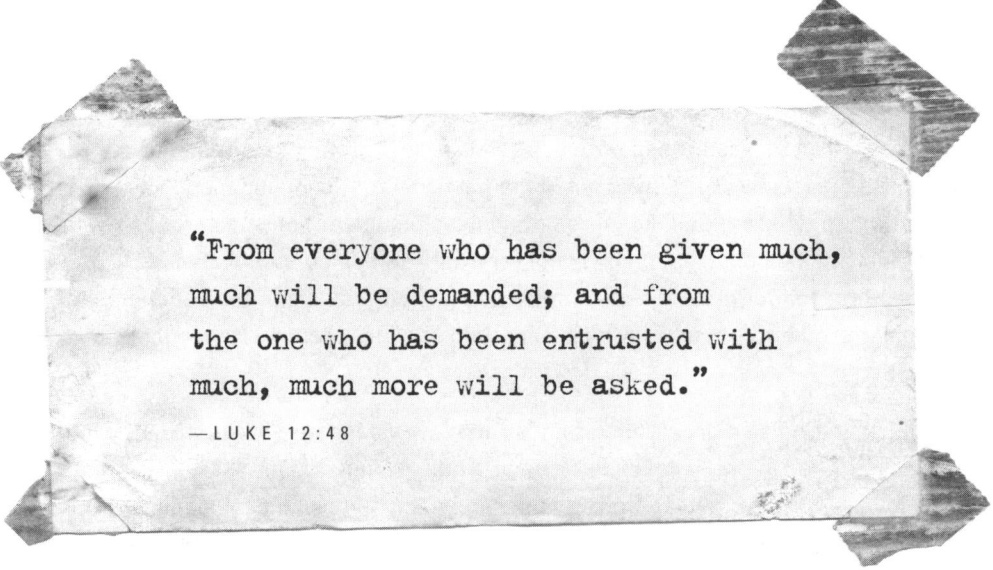

"From everyone who has been given much, much will be demanded; and from the one who has been entrusted with much, much more will be asked."

—LUKE 12:48

God on the Move

There is a lot going wrong in this world. I can't change everything. But I'm learning that God hasn't asked me to. I think there may be one little piece of the puzzle he's asking me to fill in, one good work he's asking me to do. Maybe when I'm working on my little piece and my friend is working on her little piece next to me and some church in Massachusetts is working on its piece and some Christians in Rwanda

are working on their piece…maybe then God's great masterpiece will be revealed. My piece may seem small, as if it doesn't matter, but I'm just one part of the body of Christ. God is on the move to change this world one person at a time. Olive was one small person who was loved by someone. It mattered to Olive. If Olive's mother had known, it would have mattered greatly to her. And now it matters to the children Olive is helping. What if I could be a part of something like that?

I'm convinced God is asking me to join him. God is on the move to heal, love, and restore, and he's asking, "Who will go for me?"

Who knows what God will do?

My heart cries out, "Here I am, send me."

What good works do you think God may have
prepared for you to do?

MY PRAYER

God, I thank you for where you've placed me in life, for all the good with which
you've blessed me. I know that to whom much is given, much is expected. Show
me what you expect of me, what good you have prepared for me to do for you.
Thank you for wishing to use me to bless others. Help me to humbly and joyfully
follow where you're going. Here am I. Send me.

DAY 12: WHAT IS POVERTY?

"You will always have the poor among you."
—JOHN 12:8

OK. So God has finally convinced me. I want to help; I want to jump in. So now what?

I guess the obvious question is, what exactly *is* poverty? What causes it? Why doesn't it ever seem to go away? Poverty is a big, complex animal, and what I believe about it will determine the actions I take.

So I read a lot of books. I hear a lot of opinions. I hesitate to just fill my head with a bunch of information, but I need to have some understanding of the issues. I want my actions to be informed; I want them to be effective.

Causes

I wish I could point a finger at one single thing and say, "That's it; that's to blame. Fix that and you've solved the problem." But the causes of poverty are many and inter-related, and not everyone agrees on what they are.

To begin, the natural world itself seems to conspire against us. **Natural disasters** create, aggravate, and deepen poverty. Earthquakes, flooding, hurricanes—all contribute to poverty. And often, those in poverty are affected most by natural forces, as poor housing and proximity to coasts make them especially vulnerable. I was recently staying in a nice hotel in Nairobi, Kenya, when there was a severe rainstorm. I watched, warm inside, as the rain pelted the window panes, disappointed that I couldn't go swimming that afternoon. The next morning, I read that 13 people had died in a slum just miles away, when their precariously constructed homes collapsed. What was a nuisance to me was death to them.

Other **environmental changes**—natural or man-caused—can create and reinforce poverty. Things such as climate change, deforestation, water and air pollution, and overfishing all deplete the natural resources that the poorest cling to for survival.

In Haiti, the poorest country in the Western Hemisphere, 90 percent of the land has been deforested by subsistence farmers trying to eke out a living from the land. The land is now over-farmed and makes the average farming family only $140 *per year*. Deforestation has also worsened the extent and severity of flooding, causing more deaths when natural disasters occur.

Wars cause much poverty, destroying agricultural productivity, transportation systems, hospitals, and schools, and creating refugees who are left with nothing.

Ethnic hostilities and racism cause poverty—from genocide in Rwanda to the economic effects of apartheid in South Africa.

International trade law and tariff structures prevent developing countries from gaining economic strength. In 2003, the World Bank reported that the tariffs charged on imports from developing countries were four times as high as the tariffs charged on imports from high-income countries, effectively locking out developing countries' abilities to compete in a world market.

Government corruption aggravates poverty because aid money never reaches its intended recipients.

International debt cements poverty because some developing countries with limited budgets throw the lion's share of their yearly budget to debt repayment rather than education or health care.

Social and personal sin is also at the root of some poverty. Bad life choices (often made in the context of poor education, racism, unemployment, or neglect in childhood), such as turning to drugs or alcohol, result in the poverty of individuals and their families.

Social injustice, such as discrimination against women, creates poverty through a lack of education for women (which is a key determiner of infant mortality) and through practices such as human trafficking.

A lack of education and opportunity keeps many more trapped in a cycle of poverty, without the means to do anything more than just survive.

Whew. Reading that list is exhausting, but these are just the causes if I consider poverty to be primarily an economic issue, which it isn't. All of them can be overwhelming. I can't point a finger at one thing and say, "This is to blame for poverty." And there is no one symptom I can channel my energy into in order to end poverty.

What to Do?

So if the causes of poverty are so many, and if, as Jesus said, there will always be poor among us, I want to despair. Can anything ever change? I know I need a big-picture understanding of poverty, but looking at it with a wide-angle lens overwhelms me.

But I know God is bigger than me, and God is in the business of hope, not despair. God has the power to restore lives and situations, and he, amazingly, wants to do that through me. He has good works planned for me. While I'm doing good, I might as well do strategic good. I want to make choices that will *really* help others, choices that don't just treat the symptoms of poverty or deal with one arm of it, but that are holistic and get at the root of the problem.

If someone is in need and I give him money, I may come back in a year to find the situation hasn't changed. If he has no access to education, money may not do it. He might lack the knowledge to use the money to create self-sustaining work. Or I might try to fix education, but if the environment isn't intact, my efforts won't do any good. An ancient proverb attributed to Lao Tzu says, "Give a man a fish and you feed him for a day. Teach him how to fish and you feed him for a lifetime." But this assumes the man has a pond in the first place. Or I may focus on just the spiritual needs of a person, and try to communicate the love of God to her. But as Mohandas Gandhi said, "There are people in the world so hungry that God cannot appear to them except in the form of bread." I can't ignore the physical needs in order to feed the spiritual.

The Poverty Wheel

So what matters? What needs should I tend to? If I reread those verses about the poor in the Bible, I see that *people* are what matter to God. God loves people, and he wants them whole—body, spirit, heart, mind, and soul. And for a person to be whole, a lot of factors have to work together.

Wess Stafford, in his book *Too Small to Ignore,* presents the best way of understanding it that I've found: the poverty wheel. In the center of the wheel, the hub, there is absolute poverty. The outer rim represents enough. The opposite of poverty isn't wealth—it's enough. Enough food to live, enough shelter to remain safe and dry, enough opportunity to become a self-sustaining member of society, enough dignity to be the person God created you to be. The six spokes of the wheel represent the various areas of life that must be intact for "enough" to occur. The spokes are economic, educational, health, environmental, social, and spiritual. As with an actual wheel, each spoke is necessary for the stability of the whole. When one spoke is weak, it has an impact on all the others.

• **Economic.** This is the one everyone thinks of when they think of poverty—not enough money. In many urban areas of developing nations, there are few jobs that provide adequate income for unskilled labor. More than 1 billion people—one in five—live on less than $1 per day.

• **Education.** Education equals opportunity, and without it, many stay trapped in the cycle of poverty. When education *is* present, people gain confidence and learn skills to become self-sustaining.

• **Health.** Many don't have the knowledge to keep themselves healthy and lack the resources to take care of themselves when they become ill. For example, one of the world's biggest killers is diarrhea. Mothers who haven't been educated otherwise stop giving water to children with diarrhea—thinking they have too much water in them. The children die of dehydration. Measles is still a leading cause of death in children, even though a safe vaccine has been available for 40 years. Malaria kills 1 million children each year, even though a bed net treated with insecticide that costs just $10 could save them.

• **Environment.** Each year, over 5 million children die from illnesses and other conditions caused by their environments. For example, 40 million people in Indonesia don't have access to safe drinking water, and contaminated water is one of the sources of one of the world's leading killers, diarrhea.

• **Social.** A culture or government that devalues humans deepens poverty. Child soldiers, child trafficking, a lack of education for women, unfair work practices—all are symptoms of unjust social structures and reinforce poverty.

• **Spiritual.** Few of us think of spirituality when we think of poverty, but the truth is you can be economically wealthy and spiritually poor. Poverty is a spiritual issue. Spiritual darkness causes much of the sin that creates poverty, the despair that compounds it, and our own inaction in the face of it.

Person-Focused and Holistic

When I read the Bible, I see that what ultimately matters to God is people, not circumstances or symptoms. Maybe that gives me a hint. What if my service were focused on people? And, based on the poverty wheel, what if my service could be holistic—what if it could focus not on just one spoke of that wheel, but on the person as a whole? I want to understand all the needs and circumstances of a person and seek to holistically help that person from the heart of Christ's love. It's not just about money—their lack or my extra. It's about a person, and it's about God's love.

Each of us is just one piece of the puzzle, part of the body of Christ with different functions and fulfilling different needs. The needs are many, but we are many as well. Together, the acts of these different parts of the body form a holistic ministry to the world. God has entrusted one piece of the puzzle to me, and all he asks is that I work on that one part.

Some Organizations That Attack the Roots of Poverty

Opportunity International is a Christian organization that seeks to lift people out of poverty through small loans. They educate the poor in business practices, give them loans to begin businesses, and seek to change the climate of entire communities by empowering the poor. www.opportunity.org

Compassion International holistically cares for children. They provide for physical, educational, social, health, and spiritual needs through child sponsorship and development. www.compassion.com

Healing Waters International works to reduce water-related illness and death by building self-sustaining projects that make safe drinking water accessible to the poor, while empowering local churches to bring not just physical, but also social and spiritual healing to their communities. www.healingwatersintl.org

How has your concept of poverty been challenged?
Write your thoughts and misconceptions about
poverty here.

MY PRAYER

God, please allow me to see poverty as you see it, as people you love who need help. It's so easy to get bogged down in all the causes or circumstances or politics. Give me your eyes and your love.

DAY 13: THE FACES OF POVERTY

*"Here there is no Greek or Jew,
circumcised or uncircumcised, barbarian, Scythian,
slave or free, but Christ is all, and is in all."*

—COLOSSIANS 3:11

From my comfortable position, the causes and factors of poverty are all abstract. They're far away. Poverty seems like a movie or a dream—as if the people experiencing it are just actors in a play—somehow not quite like *me,* not quite experiencing or feeling as strongly as I do. Poverty becomes a faceless cluster without personality.

But poverty is about people, and I want to experience their humanity. I want to look into the faces of poverty. The im-

Dejene, one of Kebede's nephews

poverished are just like me—no less intelligent, no less feeling. They have dreams. They make jokes. They love. They are people like my aunt. People like my neighbor. When I read their stories, I remember how very like me they are. I realize that *this* is what poverty is about. And I realize that hope lives.

Kebede

Kebede is a good man—a faithful husband and a father of a 3-year-old boy. Kebede is 30. I'm 30—an age at which life stretches out like a road of possibilities. I know a lot of couples our age with little toddlers at their side. I think of my friends with their car seats and *Dora the Explorer* DVDs, and their excitement at this new stage in life and the promise that resides in their little children.

But this 30-year-old's face is worn.

Six years ago Kebede's brother and his brother's wife died. The doctors wouldn't say from what. His brother had been like a father to him, and the pain of the loss is sharp. But what is even more painful is raising his brother's nine children. His brother left him *nine* orphans, and not knowing whether he'll be able to feed and clothe them torments Kebede each day.

"I'm depressed to see them sad, especially when I compare them to the neighbors' children who have clothes, and I can't provide food." Kebede lowers his head and begins to weep.

Thirty years old. Ten children and a wife to support. The money he makes trading grain in his remote village in Ethiopia is not nearly enough. His story isn't out of the ordinary; there are nearly 5 million orphans in Ethiopia, and one in 13 children in the developing world is an orphan.

"Sometimes I can't sleep at night. I think about how I don't have any money to feed my children." His voice cracks as he says this.

Sometimes at home in Colorado, I can't sleep at night…usually my brain is buzzing with phone calls I must remember to make and long to-do lists. But not with this. Not with fearing nightly I won't be able to feed, clothe, educate, and care for my 10 children on the few dollars I make each day.

But Kebede is persistent. Even with all his worries, he hasn't abandoned his family, as so many men in his situation have. He is determined to stay faithful to his wife. He's read the literature, and he knows his brother and sister-in-law died of AIDS, even if the doctors won't say it. As in many other regions in Africa, the social stigma of AIDS is strong—if others find out why the nine children were orphaned, they'll be ostracized, considered cursed. AIDS is kept quiet, so many in Kebede's village don't really believe it's real and take no actions to prevent it or get tested. "I tell my friends that they must be faithful to their partners. But they don't believe [AIDS] is real…I've lost my brother, my sister-in-law, and two friends to this disease. It is real."

There is hope in Kebede's story. He is determined to beat AIDS by remaining faithful to his wife and family and trying to convince other men to do the same. His family also receives support from a Compassion International Child Sponsorship Program, which provides food and necessities and an opportunity for education and spiritual growth.

He lifts the poor from the dust and the needy from the garbage dump. He sets them among princes, placing them in seats of honor. For all the earth is the Lord's, and he has set the world in order.

1 Samuel 2:8 (NLT)

But the needy will not be ignored forever; the hopes of the poor will not always be crushed.

Psalm 9:18 (NLT)

HOPE LIVES

There is also hope springing in Ethiopia. Although it still has one of the highest child mortality rates in the world, the rates have declined 40 percent in the last 15 years. The executive director of UNICEF reports that Ethiopia is making steady progress toward achieving the Millennium Development Goals, goals set in place in 2000 by a UN Millennium Summit to be met by 2015 to eradicate extreme poverty. There is still a lot of work to do. But hope lives.

Despite his circumstances, Kebede has hope. Each day as I wake up to my alarm and go for a walk in the cool Colorado air, he is out there somewhere, working hard each day, pushing for the survival of his children and hoping and believing God will deliver them.

Bineesh

It happened when Bineesh was just 8 years old.

My sister teaches 8-year-olds. It's such a wondrous age—there's so much to learn and explore. It's a time to prove yourself while still sometimes finding shelter behind your mom's safe legs.

But Bineesh didn't have the same wonder years so many of my sister's students experience. His mother, Omana, like any mother, just wanted to see her children happy. But she was a single mother. Her husband had died, leaving her with no way to provide for her family. She had a painful asthmatic condition and couldn't work. Her family's daily income was 23 cents—not nearly enough. There was no hope for remarriage—who would marry her? And even if someone wanted to marry her, how would she afford the dowry her culture expects her to provide?

Omana decided to do the only thing she knew that would take her and her children out of their misery and despair. She took Bineesh and his sister, Laca, down to

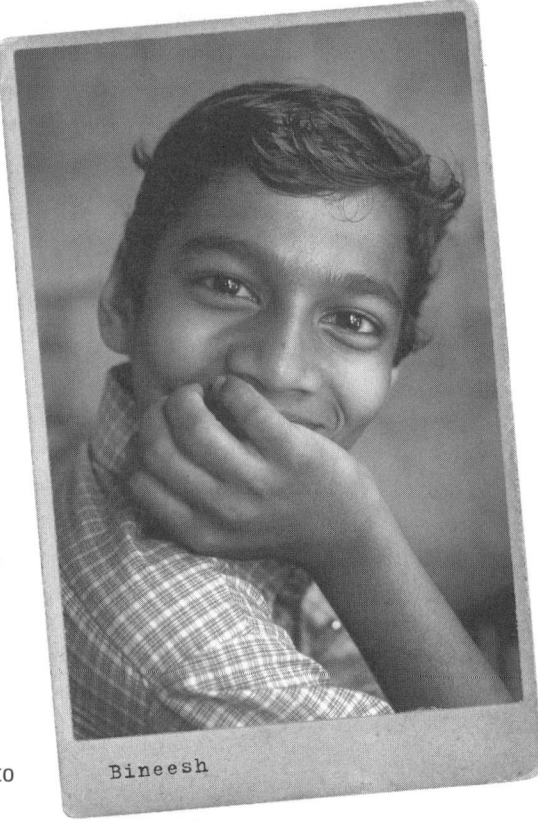

Bineesh

the river and bound them tightly to her leg with a sari. Drowning seemed better than starvation.

Trembling next to his mother's leg, Bineesh cried out, "Mama, don't kill us! One day God will bless us." And she couldn't do it. She waded out of the water, but her despair remained. A week later she got poison to put in their meager bowls of rice, still sure that the only future for her and her children was filled with suffering. But Bineesh stopped her again, crying, "One day people will see our need, and we will get blessings."

Bineesh dodged death twice at the age of 8.

I read the story, and it sounds like a fable, the story of little Bineesh in India and how he tricked death. But Bineesh in India is just like Garrett in Colorado. Or Jack in Virginia. He's not a fable; he's a real, living, breathing boy.

Bineesh's story is just one in a sea of stories of what children around the world face just to survive. Forty-one percent of the world's poor live in India, and southern India has one of the highest suicide rates among young people, as hope gives way to fatalism and despair. Over 6 million children die from malnutrition each year. And hunger isn't the worst thing facing many of the world's children: 246 million children are engaged in child labor, 126 million of them in hazardous situations. Approximately 8.4 million of these children work under horrific circumstances: forced into debt bondage or other forms of slavery, prostitution, pornography, armed conflict, or other illicit activities because of poverty. This is a dangerous world for children.

Although he had dodged death, Bineesh still had no way to survive. But even in the most seemingly hopeless of situations, hope lives. Bineesh had cried out to his mother, "One day, people will see our needs and we will get blessings!" He was right. One day, a Christian church in their area began to provide services to children in need. Omana, grasping at the only hope she'd seen in years, enrolled both of her children in the new program. Bineesh says, "If it weren't for the center, I would be dead." He and his sister now receive three meals a day. Bineesh says, "Before… there was no one to love me. Now, I get lots of love from the project staff workers! They encourage me to study hard and participate in the center's sports and arts competitions…I love to go to Sunday school. And my mom, grandma, and sister also go with me to all our church's worship services."

Now Bineesh is a vibrant 13-year-old with hope in his future. This young man is what poverty is about. This young man is what hope is about.

Zaccalot

Zaccalot was born into one of the most dangerous places possible for a child: Haiti. One in 14 infants in Haiti dies before the age of 1. Fifty-eight thousand children die each year before they reach kindergarten. Zaccalot, a shy but adorable boy with chubby cheeks, was nearly engulfed by these horrific statistics. But he wasn't, and now I can see him for what he is: not a number but a sweet creation of God.

His father is a farmer and works 12 hard hours each day. In Haiti, as in many developing countries, good farmland that can provide a sustainable income is scarce. And the number of people living in countries where cultivated land is critically scarce is projected to increase from 448 million in 2005 to between 559 million and 706 million in 2025. Zaccalot's father's 12 hours of working the land only amounts to $2 each day, the amount 1 billion people live on each day in this world. That's not enough to feed Zaccalot and his family, no matter how hard he works. It certainly isn't enough to take him to a hospital. And Zaccalot needed a hospital as a toddler. With a swollen head and a ballooned belly, Zaccalot didn't have long to live. But his father could do nothing but look on as his only son was dying. Zaccalot's mother couldn't even do that. She couldn't watch him die. So she left.

Zaccalot would have died, unnoticed by any but his parents, just another tick in the faceless count of poverty. But one day, workers from a local church program saw Zaccalot in front of his home, clearly in need of medical attention. He was taken to

Zaccalot with his mother and sister

the hospital and treated for malnourishment and worms. He was enrolled in the program, and now, three years later, he eats regular meals, plays, and learns.

Now he's a precocious little boy who loves to play soccer and loves even more to eat (a boy after my own heart). Now he's a boy with a hope for a future—for education and health and opportunity. A boy just like one I might see at the grocery store, grasping for a box of cookies or playing on the swing set, seeing how high he can go, or holding on to his mother's leg, needing love and comfort.

These faces—Kebede, Bineesh, Zaccalot—they are what poverty is all about. They are also what hope is about. They're the treasures God is restoring to the whole life he intended for each of us. They are who God wants me to care about and reach out to in his love.

Do the people in poverty seem real to you, like flesh and blood? Write about your perceptions, and perhaps misconceptions, about those in poverty.

MY PRAYER

Dear Lord, why am I so apt to just hear numbers and not see people when I'm faced with poverty? Please soften my heart. Open my eyes, even if it's painful, to see that the stories of poverty happen to real people, just like me. Help me to care and not to close my eyes or turn my head. Help me to see faces. Help me to love.

"You cannot have a more powerful word to describe the cure for poverty or for empty hearts that should be reaching out to poverty than hope."

—WESS STAFFORD

In order to understand what's at the core of poverty, I spoke with Dr. Wess Stafford, a man who knows poverty. He grew up with the poor in Africa, worked for four years with the poor in Haiti with development agencies, and has served the poor through Compassion International for 30 years (14 years as president).

What do hope and poverty have to do with each other?

Dr. Stafford: Hope is at the very core of poverty, and hope is at the very core of reaching out to the poor. Albert Einstein said, "The world is a dangerous place, not because of those who do evil, but because of those who look on and do nothing." I've worked for 30 years among the poor, and I've discovered that good people do nothing to stop poverty for only two reasons. The first is they don't know who to trust, and that's a great tragedy.

The second reason is they don't know what to do, and they become hopeless. The magnitude of the problem seems so huge, and they become paralyzed. They can't do everything, and they don't know what to do. With that level of hopelessness, even a compassionate heart tends to just get oppressed and ends up doing absolutely nothing. On the aid end of poverty, hope has got to be there, or we'll do nothing.

What about hope among those in poverty?

Dr. Stafford: For the poor, a lack of hope is at the very core of poverty. Poverty isn't about housing; it's not about sanitation; it's not about the environment. Those are all symptoms of poverty. They're the things that go wrong when poverty is around. But they're not poverty.

Poverty is kind of like having a bad fruit tree in your backyard that puts out bitter lemons. You look at the fruit and say, these lemons are totally useless—it'd be good to pick them off of that tree. Less bad fruit in the world is a good thing. But if you've hung around poverty long enough, you know even if you pick off all the bad fruit, next year the same crop of bad fruit is going to be there. We can throw ourselves at the environment or housing or whatever, but the same problems just keep cropping up year after year. That's what happens when we consider poverty to be nothing but circumstantial.

Why is this happening year after year? What's at the root of this tree that's putting out bad fruit? If you dig down to the root of the tree, you stumble onto the real root of poverty. In its essence, it is hopelessness. It's a message that says, "Nobody cares about me. Nothing works. Nobody succeeds. Everything is garbage or failure, and so am I."

The message of poverty is, "I don't matter. Nothing's going to change for me." Ultimately it's hopelessness. That's why I argue that the most strategic and loving thing you can do to fight poverty is to bring a child to her heavenly Father. It gives that child worth and a reason for hope. She thinks, "I matter because God says I matter. He knows my name and my fingerprints and each hair on my head. When a child understands that, she takes the first step out of poverty. You see this sparkle in her, this little glimmer of tenderness and hope.

Can you tell a story of a child who got this spark of hope?

Dr. Stafford: I took some major donors to a dump outside Guatemala City. I told the donors, "These are real people who live on this dump. I want you to get out of this van and talk to them. See God in these people." Everyone scattered except one man. He was so mad and said, "Wess, I'm not getting out of this van. This is nothing but destruction; this is nothing but despair. Nothing good can come from this place." So he sat in the van and stewed.

That night at the hotel, we had dinner with students in Compassion's Leadership Development Program (LDP). The students were children who had graduated from our Child Sponsorship Program. They were selected to receive a university education and Christian leadership training through LDP. About halfway through the meal, I got up, fearing this man was still mad. I came to his table with trepidation and asked, "So, how are things here?" He looked at me with tears in his eyes and a beaming smile and said, "We're at the *best* table." He motioned to the student at his table, Ari, and said, "Ask her where she grew up."

I asked Ari where she grew up, and she replied, "On the dump you visited today." I asked her what she learned from growing up on that dump. She said, "Well, Wess, I know two things. I know what it feels like when people look at you and think you're garbage. When I was 5 years old, I smelled like garbage; I wore clothes that we found in the dump. The big trucks that came to dump their garbage didn't even slow down around me. If anyone had hit me and killed me, nobody would have so much as dug a hole because, as far as they were concerned, I was already where I belonged. I was garbage, and that's how I felt."

I said, "But look at you—you're studying at the university. What else do you know?" Ari looked at me with this beautiful smile and said, "I know that *nobody* is garbage. Everybody has worth. Everyone is precious in the kingdom of God. I was there, and I am now here, *and I know that.*"

Ari was studying business administration at the college and had decided to launch a business right on the edge of that dump, a little school-supply shop. She said, "I used to find pencils in the garbage. My mom would gather up the notebooks with a few pages left and sew them together so I could go to school. I'm going to start a bookstore at the edge of that dump with affordable school supplies so that every child can have the dignity of a new notebook and pencils."

Ari went from hopelessness to hope. She discovered her worth through sponsors all the way across the world who believed in her. She discovered her worth through little successes along the way. And her hope now spills over to others—not just wanting to get out of the dump, but to help others out of it, too.

Ari's path seems to have come full circle.

Dr. Stafford: It is full circle. Stepping out of poverty is learning that I matter. If I matter, what I think matters. This is where beating back poverty happens. When a person realizes what they think matters, they gain confidence. They say, "Let me tell you what I think. Look at my community. Communities shouldn't be like that. You see how those people are treating each other? People shouldn't treat each other like that. That's what I think." Eventually they'll say, "You see this over here? This is wrong, *and I'm going to fix that.*" When a child goes from "I don't matter" to "I can fix that," you've just won the war on poverty.

Have you seen this happen?

Dr. Stafford: Compassion's founder began our work with war orphans in South Korea in 1952. The country was consumed by poverty and war, the church was virtually nonexistent, and there was nobody for these children. They'd huddle in the doorways at night to stay warm. The dump trucks would go through the streets before dawn to pick up the kids who didn't survive. They'd shake the little bundles of rags, and those who didn't make it were thrown into the truck and hauled to the landfill. You talk about hopelessness; that is the ultimate in despair.

We ministered there for 20 years, and then we knew it was time to pull out. The government was strong, and it was no longer a developing nation—they no longer needed our help. The pastors and leaders of the country came to me and said, "Wess, we can take care of ourselves now. But only half the story has been told—the half where we received. Come back, and let us now give."

We had a banquet to relaunch Compassion in South Korea in 2003—this time for them to give to others. It was amazing—500 leaders of the church were there. I got up to give a talk on Compassion, and about 10 minutes into it, a man got up and waved his hand. I called on him, and he said, "You don't have to tell us this. I'm one of your kids.
I grew up through Compassion's programs. I am the head of the Salvation Army in South Korea." A guy over in a corner jumped up and said, "Yep, I'm the head of the Nazarene church, and I grew up with Compassion." And they popped up all across this auditorium with these stories. The very kids we ministered to are now the backbone of society, the backbone of the church. I could introduce you to 300 sponsored Korean children who became pastors—some of churches with 20,000 people. At one church meeting of 10,000 people, we shared the ministry of Compassion, and 4,000 people decided to sponsor children—in one morning. They know poverty; they know what it feels like to leave it behind. And they know that to whom much is given, much is required. Hope has been brought to their nation, and they are ready to give back.

This hope came out of absolute hopelessness in the doorways. South Korea has come full circle. Now you're back to the bad fruit on the tree. These changed lives are the ones changing that fruit. You change the life of a child, you change a family. You change a family, you change a church. You change a church, you change a community. You change communities, you change a nation.

Hope is in the center of it all. You cannot have a more powerful word to describe the cure for poverty or for empty hearts that should be reaching out to poverty than *hope*.

Do you have hope for those in poverty and your
part in reaching out? Why or why not?

MY PRAYER

Dear Lord, please fill me with your hope. I don't want to be a cynic about poverty, because I know you're not. I know you want to transform people and situations. I know you have hope and plans for me and those living in poverty. Please fill me with your Holy Spirit and with your hope for this world. Please help me to be your messenger of hope in this world.

*"It's the greatest poverty to decide that
a child must die so that you may live as you wish."*

—MOTHER TERESA

Not Against Flesh and Blood

It can seem to me (especially when I fill my head full of academic opinions and statistics) that poverty just results from flaws in politics and people and circumstances and environment. But then a verse jumps into my head: "Our struggle is not against flesh and blood, but against the rulers, against the authorities, against the powers of this dark world and against the spiritual forces of evil in the heavenly realms" (Ephesians 6:12). There truly is evil afoot in this world. Wess Stafford, having worked among the poor for decades, deeply understands the spiritual dimension of poverty. When I interviewed him, he said this regarding Satan's plot in poverty:

Satan is in the business of breaking God's heart. He's not stupid, and he watched Creation. He watched all the way up to day six before he saw the chink in God's armor. On day six he finally sees God create man. This time he doesn't just speak the creation into existence, but God fashions man from his own hands. He breathes into him, steps back, and says, "Wow! That is really, really good." And I'm convinced Satan was standing on the sidelines, looking on, thinking, "There it is; that's the chink in his armor. He loves mankind, and if I want to break his heart, his agenda, then I'm going to attack what he loves most." So when do you attack? He's not stupid. He knows that the younger, the better. He whispers to children through poverty: "You don't matter."

I remember Ari, the girl who grew up on the trash dump. Satan's goal wasn't just to destroy her physically. It was to destroy her soul: to convince her that she didn't matter, that no one loved her, that God didn't care, and that she was garbage. The most important thing—what God cares about and what Satan wants to destroy—is a person's soul, a soul like Ari's. I need to be ever mindful that poverty isn't just about AIDS. It's not about clean water. It's not about a lack of safe housing. It's not about poor educational programs. It's not about lack of sanitation.

It's about souls.

It's about a boy orphaned by AIDS, without parents to love him and tell him he matters. It's about a man who feels no dignity or purpose because he's never had the education or opportunity to be who God created him to be. It's about a woman who buries her soul and sells herself because she feels she has no other choice and doesn't matter anyway.

People matter. God created each unique soul and loves each one and has a purpose for each one—even if that individual is living in a slum surrounded by darkness, filth, and despair. God has as much a plan for people in poverty—*every single one*—as he does for me.

The Greatest Poverty

I shudder to think that when talking about poverty and my role in reaching out to others, I might sound arrogant, like some imperialist who, in my presumed superiority, condescends to help those "poor, poor souls."

That's hardly the case. I may not be doing much better than those in poverty myself. I've seen poor people worship, and they've definitely got me beat there. The poor thirst for God more than I do. They call out to him more than I do. Sometimes I suspect they love him more than I do. My faith seems cold and stiff next to theirs. No, I'm certainly not some kind of superior benefactor.

I, too, am embroiled in a battle. All of us are. For while there is a poverty of too little, there is also a poverty of too much. Satan can squash souls by making them believe they are insignificant and alone. But Satan can also entwine and imprison *my* soul in the poverty of too much.

I don't always feel rich, but I am. And riches are an equally potent, if not more potent, weapon to ensnare a soul. The poverty of too much can freeze my heart. It can deaden compassion. It can paralyze hands. Mother Teresa saw an awful lot of poverty—horrible poverty—and still decided *this* was the greatest poverty: "to decide that a child must die so that you may live as you wish."

I am in the greatest poverty, a poverty of my soul, when I eat my fill and lounge on my couch, while thinking only fleetingly of others not as materially blessed as I have been. My poverty is real when my love is deadened, medicated, frozen by *too much*. And my soul is maybe in even more danger than those in the poverty of too little.

I am no great emissary kindly bringing restoration to *those* people. No. I am simply a fellow human, given a different responsibility and role to play on this earth. God placed me where I am, and he placed others where they are. The goal isn't for others to become like me, a wealthy American. The goal is simply for everyone to have enough. Those in poverty need enough—enough food each day, enough clean water to lead a healthy life, enough dignity to be the masterpiece God created them to be. And for me, straying closer to the poverty of too much, I need to move further back toward enough, to use what I have been given to help lift others toward enough, to use my resources to love as Jesus loved.

Incomparably Great Power

And while I'm remembering this is a spiritual battle—that I'm struggling against the dark powers of this world—I can't forget the other side of the battle, or I'll be overtaken with despair.

Graciously, God pops another verse into my head: "Know the hope to which [God] has called you…and his incomparably great power for us who believe. That power is like the working of his mighty strength, which he exerted in Christ when he raised him from the dead" (Ephesians 1:18-20). It's not just human problems we're struggling against, but it's also not just human power that we've been given. Our hope and our power come from God, the same power that seated Jesus "far above all rule and authority, power and dominion" (Ephesians 1:21).

When I think of trying to do anything to help those in need or stop the evil powers at work, I'm afraid. But the same "incomparably great" power that God exerted to raise Christ from the dead, *that same power* is what God has for us who believe. Wow. The powers of this world don't even compare to the power of God. God is serious about using me in this world.

I'm not left alone to figure out this complicated issue of poverty by myself. God has given me all I need to fulfill the good works he has planned—his hope and his power in prayer and action. Satan recognizes the spiritual potential of poverty, but I recognize the incomparable power God has for us who believe.

The Hope of Ephantus

I witnessed the power and hope of God in a slum in Nairobi, Kenya. The slum perches on the edge of the bulging city dump, and driving past, we saw people bending over the rank garbage, scavenging. Another man was passed out in the pile. As our bus bumped through the crowded streets, glazed-over and hard eyes stared in at us. When we arrived at the church, which hosts a Child Sponsorship Program though Compassion International, the atmosphere sparked—we didn't see the hard eyes of the street anymore, but heard the joyful, energetic voices of children greeting us with a sign reading "Jesus loves you."

Inside the church, a young man, Ephantus, told his story.

My name is Ephantus, and I am here today as a testimony that the labor of Compassion and the many sponsors who commit money and write letters is not in vain. I was born into a family of four. My dad was a drunkard, but my mom was a committed Christian. She would take us to church while my dad went to the bar to down a drink or two. At church, we were told that God loves us, but we couldn't connect with what love was. We didn't experience love in our home.

Then one day an opportunity came, Compassion came. I got a sponsor, a man called Jack MacDonald, a man who will always be in my heart. For 11 years he was committed to writing me and sending money to sponsor me—a person I've never met. To see that somebody 8,000 miles away would commit to make sure that I went to school and dressed nicely and had my hospital bills paid—that is where I first saw love. My heart started understanding what my Sunday school teacher told me about love, and I gave my life to the Lord.

When I was 15, I got my first Christmas card. Mr. Jack MacDonald wished me a merry Christmas. It blew me away that somebody cared so much to send me a card. That was over 10 years ago, and I still keep that card with me. Today I understand what love is. I've never seen God, but I know love because my sponsor, whom I have never seen, has shown me love.

Ephantus

My daddy was still drinking. He would come home with a hangover and sit, wondering, "Who are these good people who would buy my son clothes and gifts? Who are these people who are so good?" That kept pricking his conscience. One Saturday he got very drunk and went to bed. On Sunday morning he woke up and said, "Today I want to go to church." From that day, my dad has never missed church a single Sunday. Today he is a preacher and is drunk by the Holy Spirit—because somebody from the U.S. cared enough to sponsor a child. Because of my sponsor's love, my entire family was transformed.

There are millions of children in Africa who never get an opportunity. But even though the statistics are like the book of Lamentations, I thank God because there is another story. Lives are being transformed because people are giving us encouragement, committing to see us achieve something in life.

Know that your labor is not in vain. I am just one in a multitude. This project is life for us. For our family it meant my salvation, my education, my health, and my father's salvation. We have hope because of Compassion.

I have now committed my life to minister to young people. It's my joy to care for them, to show them love, to pray with them. The harvest out here is truly plenty, and we are seeing lives transformed. If your mission is just for a year, plant corn; if it is for five years, plant something that will grow for five years; but if it is for a lifetime, plant people.

Do you agree that poverty is a spiritual issue? If so, how do you think this affects you personally? Write here your reflections after today's reading.

Dear God, thank you for the hope you have given me in Christ and for the incomparably great power you have for me. I praise you that you love this world and the people in it. Thank you that you haven't left us alone in this world to fend for ourselves, but are with us, helping us. Please fill me with your Holy Spirit and your power that I might pray and reach out in your power.

Week Three
Reflection Questions

What was the most challenging truth you struggled with this week?

How has your perspective on poverty changed this week?

How do you think hope relates to poverty?

Do you believe you are involved in a spiritual battle yourself? In what ways?

Action Steps

1. Take some time to learn a little more about poverty this week. If there is a particular issue that tugs at your heart, spend some time researching it. Or visit informational Web sites, such as www.unicef.org, www.worldbank.org, www.one.org, or www.compassion.com/child-advocacy.

2. Spend some extra time (on your own or in a group) praying that God would prepare and transform your heart to jump in to love this world. God is looking for people to join him at "such a time as this." Commit yourself to joining him.

3. Poverty is about people. Spend time this week with someone in need; look into the face of poverty and listen.

4. Hope lives. Spend time spreading hope—discuss with friends the hope that you have for this world and the role you can play in it.

PRAYER

PRAYER IS THE WEAPON God has given us for the journey of loving and serving those in need. This week of prayer and journaling will help us explore the power of prayer in a world in need of restoration and help us make prayer a part of daily life.

HOPE LIVES

The great business of
the church is prayer.
And the greatest need
of a needy world is a
praying church.

DAY 16: THE GREAT BUSINESS OF THE CHURCH

"The great business of the church is prayer.
And the greatest need of a needy world is a praying church."
—ERIC ALEXANDER

" 'Because of the oppression of the weak and the groaning
of the needy, I will now arise,' says the Lord.
'I will protect them from those who malign them.' "
—PSALM 12:5

I know what Ephantus would say if you asked him what changed his daddy and what changed his family. It was God, it was the love shared by others, and it was prayer. Ephantus, his entire family, and his sponsor were dedicated to praying for Ephantus' father. And if you ask Ephantus' father, he'll tell you: Prayer works. The battle of poverty is a spiritual battle, and one of the most powerful weapons we've been outfitted with, in fact our *incomparably* powerful weapon, is prayer. If this battle were only against the material world, we would throw ourselves into programs. But if poverty is a struggle "not against flesh and blood, but against the rulers, against the authorities, against the powers of this dark world and against the spiritual forces of evil in the heavenly realms" (Ephesians 6:12), then we also throw ourselves into prayer.

The Essential Work

"Pray *continually*" (1 Thessalonians 5:17, emphasis added). "Pray in the Spirit *on all occasions* with all kinds of prayers and requests. With this in mind, be alert and *always keep on praying* for all the saints" (Ephesians 6:18, emphasis added). Prayer is not just a thoughtful thing I do on the side, as I do the "real" work of helping others; prayer *is* the work. I want my thinking to become like Scottish theologian Eric Alexander's: "In all our thinking about Christian service, prayer needs to become fundamental instead of supplemental…Prayer is the work; it is the essence of the task to which we are called, and apart from it, all other work, and I mean Christian work, is a sheer waste of time and energy divorced from the basic work of prayer. Everything else is insignificant."

When I look at Scripture, it's clear that God chooses to act when he hears our cries for help. In Genesis 18, God chose to act against Sodom and Gomorrah because of the outcry that reached him, not only because of the cities' sexual sins but because they ignored the poor and needy (Ezekiel 16:49). God chose to act to save Lot as a result of Abraham's pleas for his family. God also chose to rescue the Israelites from slavery because he heard their cries to him (Exodus 3:7-8). God *listens* to prayers, and he chooses to use them to change the world around us.

God could certainly run this world without my prayers for those in need, but for some reason he has given me, given each of us, the great honor of affecting change in this world through prayer. It's as if Shakespeare suddenly decided to start talking to his characters, allowing Hamlet to have sway over the plot of his great masterpiece. I love how Pascal, the French mathematician, put it: "God has instituted prayer so as to confer upon His creatures the dignity of being causes." God doesn't have to work through prayers to restore this world, but he's chosen to honor me as his masterpiece created to do good works—how could I not pray?

Spiritual Giants

But I must admit that a voice whispers in my head that powerful, world-changing prayer is just spiritually out of my league. My faith seems far too small to affect any change in this world so full of needs that are so much bigger than me. What if nothing happens? Isn't serious, committed prayer for this world really the domain of the spiritual giants? The zealous ascetics who can pray all night, the 85-year-old widows who seem to have a direct line to God, the great church leaders whose golden prayers seem to come so easily—these are the people whose prayers matter. I'm simply not like that; I'm tempted to just leave it to them.

George Müller definitely seems like one of those spiritual giants. He founded five orphanages in England in the 1800s, ensuring that 10,000 children were clothed, fed, and educated. He never asked for money to operate the orphanages, but instead, through the power of prayer, relied on God to provide monetarily for the ministry. And God did. I look at Mr. Müller and think, "I could never be like him; he was clearly gifted with prayer and faith."

Müller thought otherwise. He wrote passionately against thinking that the power of prayer is unleashed only to the super-spiritual: "Do not think that I am an extraordinary believer," he said, "having privileges above any other of God's dear children. Give it a try! Stand still in the hour of trial, and you will see the help of God." He also said, "Although every believer is not called upon to establish orphanages or charities and trust in the Lord for the support of these institutions, all believers are called upon to cast all their burdens upon Him…and expect answers to their petitions according to his will." Müller insisted that he wasn't a spiritual giant. He insisted that he didn't have a special gift for prayer but simply relied on the power available to *all* of us. Even to a doubter like me.

Elijah is another guy who definitely seems out of my league spiritually. But the book of James says, "Elijah was a man just like us. He prayed earnestly that it would not rain, and it did not rain on the land for three and a half years" (James 5:17). Just like us…*just like me?* That's hard to believe. But there it is, written in the Bible. Directly before this statement, James says, "The prayer of a righteous man is powerful and effective" (James 5:16). My prayers for this world in need are classified the same as Elijah's—powerful and effective.

> "We do not wage war as the world does.
> The weapons we fight with are not
> the weapons of the world.
> On the contrary, they have divine
> power to demolish strongholds."
> —2 CORINTHIANS 10:3-4

Helpless

I feel utterly unqualified to pray to change the world. I'm not a George Müller. I'm not an Elijah. But I find a story Jesus tells in Luke 18 to be of great comfort to my unqualified soul. A religious teacher prayed to God, full of his own accomplishments, and a "sinner" prayed to God, empty and destitute before God. The second man wasn't a great theologian, not even a man with his spiritual life together and his words perfectly prepared. And yet, Jesus said, it was that weak, empty man whose prayer was heard.

Thank God. Prayer is the great equalizer. It doesn't belong just to those with titles and tidy spiritual lives. It belongs to those who come empty to God to be used. " 'My grace is sufficient for you, for my power is made perfect in weakness' " (2 Corinthians 12:9). All along, my eyes have been too much on myself, on my weakness and lack of faith. But prayer is putting my trust in heavenly power—the incomparable power available to us—rather than my own abilities or strength. Thank God again. It isn't about me. It's about an imperfect, finite creature crying out for the aid of an infinite, powerful God who *wants* to restore this world.

I love the paradox of Christianity—God lends his unimaginable power to those who would be the least in this world otherwise: the poor, the widow, and the orphan. On the surface, it looks as if those trapped in poverty have absolutely no power to effect any change whatsoever; they're helpless. And I, too, can feel absolutely helpless and trapped in inaction when faced with the paralyzing facts of poverty. But Christianity is at home with helplessness. According to the Norwegian theologian Ole Hallesby, the great ingredient for prayer *is* helplessness. "Prayer and helplessness are inseparable," he says. "Only those who are helpless can truly pray."

I'll have learned to *truly* pray when I know my absolute insufficiency and helplessness in facing this world. When I cry out to God from this spot, I am like the Israelite slaves whom God pitied and the "poor in spirit" whom God blesses. How generous God is! Prayer isn't the domain of the experts or the spiritual supermen; it's the domain of anyone weak enough to throw aside the measures of the world and say, "God, I'm helpless, and I cry out to you."

Faith

My lifestyle, packed with material goods, can make the immaterial—faith and the power of prayer—seem flimsy and fictitious. Prayer seems like smoke that wafts up from my lips and quickly drifts away on the wind, unheard and aimless. The poor have an edge on me; God has chosen them to be rich in faith (James 2:5). The second great ingredient to prayer, after helplessness, is faith, according to Hallesby. I need to learn from the poor—Christians living in poverty can't rely on material security but must rely on God's promises. God's goodness is thick and close as, out of necessity, they're used to looking through the grim realities of this world to the truth of the spiritual world. Ephantus, his mother, and his siblings couldn't rely on a cozy paycheck from their father, a hot meal on the table, or warm sweaters on their backs. They only had God to turn to. When they pray, they pray with urgency. They pray hard. They pray believing it will make a real difference. That's what I need. As I bow my head to pray, I need to see beyond my oak table, my bowl of steaming ravioli, and my prayer like smoke—to put my trust in the incomparable power of God.

Jesus says I can move a mountain if I just have faith the size of a mustard seed (Matthew 17:20-21). If I need faith the size of a mustard seed to move a mountain, my faith must be smaller than a speck of dust. I sponsor a boy in India named Sathy who loves soccer and studying languages. He recently wrote to say that his father is often drunk, never working, and has left his family. My heart cracks. This dear boy without a father. I remember Ephantus and his faith—he prayed his father would stop drinking and come back to the family. And he did. I pray for hope and faith like Ephantus'. My faith seems insufficient to move even an anthill of poverty, let alone a mountain.

I suppose that's a good place to start. If I'm helpless, I'm forced to cry out to God in my lack of faith. Jesus said, "Anything is possible if a person believes" to a father who asked Jesus to heal his sick son. The man cried back, "I do believe, but help me overcome my unbelief!" (Mark 9:23-24, NLT). Amen, brother. That's how I feel. Jesus must have granted this man extra faith, for Jesus healed his son. The essence of faith is to simply approach Christ, even if I approach to simply ask for more faith. I, like the father with a sick son, must cry out to Jesus, *"Lord, I believe you want to work through my prayers to restore Sathy's father. Please help me with my unbelief!"*

I hear the words of Hallesby as a rally cry:

"The work of praying is prerequisite to all other work in the kingdom of God, for the simple reason that it is by prayer that we couple the powers of heaven to our helplessness…the powers which can capture strongholds and make the impossible possible."

God's power and my helplessness make the impossible possible in this world in need of restoration.

In My Own Words

Pray through the following psalm, and devote yourself and your heart to God and ask him to hear your prayers.

Hear, O Lord, and answer me,
for I am poor and needy.
Guard my life, for I am devoted to you.
You are my God; save your servant
who trusts in you.

Have mercy on me, O Lord,
for I call to you all day long.
Bring joy to your servant,
for to you, O Lord,
I lift up my soul.
You are forgiving and good, O Lord,
abounding in love to all who call to you.

Hear my prayer, O Lord;
listen to my cry for mercy.
In the day of my trouble I will call to you,
for you will answer me.

Among the gods there is none like you, O Lord;
no deeds can compare with yours.
All the nations you have made
will come and worship before you, O Lord;
they will bring glory to your name.
For you are great and do marvelous deeds;
you alone are God.

Teach me your way, O Lord,

and I will walk in your truth;

give me an undivided heart,

that I may fear your name.

I will praise you, O Lord my God, with all my heart;

I will glorify your name forever.

For great is your love toward me;

you have delivered me from the depths of the grave.

The arrogant are attacking me, O God;

a band of ruthless men seeks my life—

men without regard for you.

But you, O Lord, are a compassionate and gracious God,

slow to anger, abounding in love and faithfulness.

Turn to me and have mercy on me;

grant your strength to your servant

and save the son of your maidservant.

Give me a sign of your goodness,

that my enemies may see it and be put to shame,

for you, O Lord, have helped me and comforted me.

—Psalm 86

DAY 17: APPROACHING GOD

"In him and through faith in him we may approach God with freedom and confidence."
—EPHESIANS 3:12

"Pray continually."
—1 THESSALONIANS 5:17

Praying in the Shower

Prayer is important, and God will work through prayer to deliver those in need—that much is clear from what I've read in the Bible. But prayer is still baffling. How do I approach God? How do I do it continually? I want to develop a life of praying for others that is natural. If I'm going to pray without ceasing, it should be something that flows out of me organically, not just something reserved for Tuesday night prayer meetings. But how exactly do I do that?

My relationship with God often seems like a paradox. He is both the Lord of the universe, at whose feet I would fall if faced with his glory, and at the same time he's the Lord who called me *friend*. If I'm praying without ceasing, chatting away in the shower, it seems that I'm praying to the Lord who calls me friend...but what about the other side of it? Christ is my friend, but he's also a God of infinite holiness. How do I reconcile the infinite grandeur of God with the intimacy required by constant prayer?

In my church upbringing, I've learned to be casual with Christ. I pray when the thought crosses my mind, when I'm driving, as I watch TV. And that's great. That, to me, is organic. But I never want to forget to *whom* I'm praying—not a short-order cook taking orders for the poor, but the almighty God. I can approach God "with freedom and confidence," but I want to do this with awe, not flippantly.

On the other hand, as C. S. Lewis once wrote, "It would be better not to be reverent at all than to have a reverence which denied the proximity." So can I pray reverently in the shower? I think so…but maybe my question is beside the point. Prayer isn't a formula or a legalistic contract I enter into with God. Prayer is a relationship—a constant relationship, like breathing.

The Divine Incognito

But who am I kidding? My issue most of the time isn't whether I'm approaching God correctly. The *real* issue is remembering to seek God, getting around to approaching him at all.

> "We may ignore, but we can nowhere evade, the presence of God.
> The world is crowded with Him.
> He walks everywhere *incognito*.
> And the *incognito* is not always hard to penetrate. The real labour is to remember, to attend.
> In fact, to come awake.
> Still more, to remain awake."
>
> —C. S. LEWIS

To come awake and to remain awake. That's the real challenge. Praying constantly is remaining awake to God's presence. I want to make praying a habit, so I test things out. I try praying in the morning. Praying while walking. Praying on my commute. Praying on my knees. Finding one spot to return to again and again to pray. Maybe in doing so, it will become natural. Much like when lovers meet on a particular path and the path becomes a place of deep meaning and nostalgia, I cultivate my place with God. A place that immediately reminds me of the Divine Incognito always beside me. My prayers are awakening me to the truth of God's infinite presence.

As I develop an organic, flowing prayer life with God, praying for the needs of others becomes more like breathing—something that just happens naturally. It starts as an intentional habit and slowly is evolving into an involuntary reaction. As I enjoy an ice cream cone on a sunny day, I remember to thank God for the day and the cone…and to pray that God would provide enough for my friend Thabitha in Kenya and fill her life with beauty. Perhaps eventually, as I enjoy my nice, hot shower, I'll remember to thank God for his kindness in such luxury…*and* pray for those so in need of clean water.

Prayer and Action

A life of continual prayer leads to more than just continual prayer. Not only does God work through prayer to change this world, God works through prayer to change *me*. When prayer is an organic part of my life, it will change my heart and it will spark my actions. I can hardly enjoy my ice cream cone, pray for Thabitha, and then move on. I'd be like the man James spoke of who sees his brother hungry, says "Go, I wish you well; keep warm and well fed" (James 2:16), and moves on without helping. If my prayer were at all sincere, I'd have to act. C. S. Lewis commented that it is sometimes so much easier to pray for a bore than to go and visit him—that sometimes we may be praying *instead of* doing. And sometimes I *can* view prayer as my easy out—a Get Out of Jail Free card. If I pray, I've done my good deed and can move on. But "faith by itself, if it is not accompanied by action, is dead" (James 2:17). If I have a living faith and I'm praying sincerely, my prayers will breed action.

Sincere prayer will change my heart. The Holy Spirit will steadily transform me and trade my thoughts for God's. I'll begin to be filled more and more with God's love for others. I'll begin to care more and more about Thabitha and what happens to her. God's Holy Spirit will help me not only to keep on praying for her but also to do something to help her.

The Great Motivator

And it doesn't stop there. Praying continually doesn't just change what I do—it changes why I do it. Not only does God use prayer to motivate me to act, God uses prayer to help me love. God uses prayer to change my motivation from guilt or duty to love. I've seen how vital it is that my service to those in need be done in love—not in guilt or duty or condescension. Prayer changes motives.

I'm messed up. Even with the best intentions, my motivations and ways meander. I start well—I really want to help that one girl I know. And I end badly—I really want praise for what I've done. I start badly—I give money because I feel guilty. And I end well—I learn humility from those I serve. It's a good thing we've got God. On my own, I'll botch it up. But God's Holy Spirit straightens my meanderings. He changes my motivation to his—love. And it doesn't happen through my happy thoughts and hard concentration. God does it through prayer. Love becomes my banner and motivator through the Holy Spirit changing me as I pray continually.

I can never rely simply on my human capacity for love and compassion—it wears thin so quickly. I've gone through empty times of faith, when my love for others was as cold and hard as the Colorado ground in winter. But in these times, *God's* love carries me to the other side. His love doesn't fade as my emotions ebb. How exactly does that happen? I don't really know; it's one of the mysteries of God. What I do know is that when I find myself in these times of hardness, I realize that I've been relying on my own ability to love others and have forgotten to seek God and ask him for his help. When I turn to God and ask him for his love, he restores and refreshes me. When I ask God for his love to be my foundation and motivation, he builds a foundation that doesn't crack.

Love is the center of it all. We serve others because we love them. And we love them because Christ first loved us. We pray for people because we love them. And we learn to love them by praying for them. I can't depend on my own love; it's God's love that transforms and restores. I must go to God in prayer, to be strengthened by his Word and by his Holy Spirit. So I see that prayer is absolutely essential if I want to love and serve others for the long haul. Prayer brings everything back to the center— to God and his love and his healing for this world. God's great motivator—love—will become my banner as his Holy Spirit moves in me and in this world through prayer.

"Faith works by love, faith is energized by love, and the life of faith is a life that is active because of love . . . it is love that alone really gives power and strength in the Christian life."
—MARTYN LLOYD-JONES

Describe how you would like your prayer life to be. How do you think that would affect your love for others?

MY PRAYER

Dear Lord, I praise you, for you are, at once, the holy God of the universe and my friend. I praise you because you are always with me, you are always listening to my prayers. I want praying to become like breathing. Please help me to come awake to your infinite presence. I pray that your Holy Spirit will make me like you and will enable me to love others with your love. Thank you for this gift.

DAY 18: MAKING A HABIT OF IT

"Pray continually."

—1 THESSALONIANS 5:17

Prayer Ideas

We want to be devoted to prayer, and devotion takes thought and planning. It's good to have a plan of attack for prayer—Satan will certainly have a plan of attack to distract us from prayer. Each unique person's prayer life will look as different as each person looks. Some people like a structured prayer routine; others prefer a more organic, open-ended prayer life. The direction you take in your prayer life is entirely personal. There's no most holy way to do it. Pray to determine what path is right for you.

Here are ways to develop a habit of praying for those in need. Consider what fits your lifestyle and your personality best.

Personal Prayer

- **Commit to pray for those in need at the same time each day for a set period of time.** You could decide to pray one minute, five minutes, 15 minutes (or even longer if you wish) each day. Set a specific time or place you'll pray—each morning as you wake, at night before you turn off the light, on your drive to work, at noon, while you shower—something that you do each day. You could even set an alarm or your watch to go off at the same time each day to remind you.

- **Build longer times of prayer into your schedule.** Once a week or once a month, you could spend half an hour (or longer) in prayer for specific needs in the world.

- **Plan what you'll pray for.** An easy way to do this is to have a small notebook that can fit into your pocket. In it, write down what you'll pray for each day of the week. For example, you could pray for a specific person or region of the world each day. Or you could pray for a different need in the world each day, such as child labor, AIDS, war, the persecuted church, and so on. As you think of things you want to remember to pray for, add them to different days in your notebook. You can also integrate this prayer into your regular prayer—each day, pray through the different spheres of your life. On Monday, pray for your family. On Tuesday, pray for your friends and co-workers. On Wednesday, pray for your church. On Thursday, pray for your community. On Friday, pray for your country. On Saturday, pray for a need abroad.

- **Pray specifically.** It's so much easier to pray fervently when saying, "God, please heal Josephine from her infection," rather than "God, please help those who are suffering." You can sign up to be a prayer partner for Compassion International and pray for specific prayer requests that Compassion has received from abroad. Each day, you'll have one specific person or situation to spend a couple of moments in prayer for. Visit www.compassion.com/sponsordonor/ prayerpartner to sign up.

- **Pray for things you're passionate about.** We don't each have to pray for every need out there. Maybe you'll want to dedicate yourself to praying for orphans; maybe you'll want to pray for social justice for women in developing countries; maybe you'll want to pray for one specific country that's close to your heart. Each day or each week, you can pray for a different aspect of this need.

- **Pray in a structured way.** You may commit to pray regularly for one specific person (for example, if you sponsor a child in another country). But sometimes we just don't know what to pray! We run out of ideas and just start repeating, "God, please bless Beth." If you want to pray in a more structured way for your one person, visit www.compassion.com/sponsordonor/prayerpartner/waystopray, which will give you one thing to focus on praying for that person each week of the year.

- **Pray for the larger body of Christ.** "Be persistent in your prayers for all believers everywhere" (Ephesians 6:18, NLT). Consider signing up for Voice of the Martyrs' weekly updates and monthly newsletters to use as a prayer guide for persecuted Christians around the world at www.persecution.com. If your church supports missionaries or has an international sister church, ask to receive their prayer requests.

Fasting

Another spiritual discipline you can practice along with prayer is fasting, abstaining from food for a set period of time. In the book of Esther, we read how Esther and her maids, along with all of the Jews in Susa, fasted for three days before Esther approached the king to attempt to stop the genocide of the Jews. We read in Acts how the early church fasted in order to dedicate something to God (Acts 13; 14). How you decide to implement a fast is up to you. It's a very personal discipline between you and God.

Fasting can make your prayers for others all the more urgent and remind you to rely on God. Each time you feel a hunger pain, you're reminded to say a prayer for whatever you've decided to pray for, and you'll feel the urgency of the needs of others. Fasting can also help you realize just how reliant on God you are and remember that God is our provider. Here are some ideas for fasting:

- **Fast during lunch** (eating breakfast and dinner, but no snacks in between). Set aside the half hour or hour you would usually spend on lunch and commit it to prayer. Find a quiet, empty room, or take a walk or sit in your car.

  Consider making a lunch-hour fast a regular habit. You could commit to fast every first Thursday of the month or even every Monday. (You won't be so focused on how bad *your* Monday is if you're dedicated to praying for others!) Place the money you save in a jar, and at the end of several months, use it to take someone downcast out to dinner or give it to a food bank or an organization such as Bread for the World (www.bread.org).

- **Abstain from one specific item or activity.** For example, abstain from Starbucks or sweets or TV—something that normally takes your time and attention. (For me it would be weekly trips for ice cream!) Then turn this attention toward God. For example, if you spend 15 minutes every couple of days driving to get coffee, consider giving this up for a set period of time and using the time to pray instead (and using the money to help others). Or abstain from 30 minutes of playing video games or 30 minutes of television for a set time period, and use that time in prayer.

- **Fast on a Saturday or over a weekend,** for a longer commitment to prayer and fasting. Pray for an hour or two on Friday or Saturday night, or go to a peaceful place during the day for an extended prayer time.

- **Ask friends or family or a church small group to join you in fasting.** It's always easier to maintain a commitment when you're doing it with a group. You can also set up a time to pray together as a group.

- **Mirror Jesus by fasting for 40 days.** Check out *A Call to Die* by David Nasser, a devotional that leads you through a 40-day fast.

Praying With Others

"If two of you agree here on earth concerning anything you ask, my Father in heaven will do it for you. For where two or three gather together as my followers, I am there among them" (Matthew 18:19-20, NLT). There's just something special about a group of Christ followers joining in prayer together, beyond what we experience in prayer alone. Praying with the body of Christ will create a bond with other Christians, maintain your zeal, and keep you accountable.

If you're already part of a prayer group, consider adding prayer for those in need to your list. If you're not part of a prayer group, consider starting one or joining one. Meet as often as you like: once a week, once a month, or quarterly. (Or hold a one-time prayer meeting.) You can pray for 15 minutes over lunch or all night. If there's a need you feel especially compelled to pray for, such as orphans or AIDS, focus on that one need. If you start a prayer group that meets regularly, choose specific aspects of each topic to pray for at each meeting.

The next two days' readings will be extended times of prayer and journaling. Consider fasting on one or both of these days.

Take time to consider how you would like to make prayer a greater part of your daily life. Write your commitment here.

Write here how you'd like to make prayer for others a part of your daily life:

Write here how you'd like to make fasting a part of your prayer life for others:

Write here how you'd like to make praying with others a part of your prayer life:

MY PRAYER

Dear Lord, thank you for your gift of prayer. Thank you for allowing me to be involved in your great work of restoring this world. Help me to be devoted to prayer. Use your Holy Spirit to urge me in prayer. Help me determine what steps I might take to make prayer a regular habit. And use my prayer to change me to be more like you.

"In the same way, the Spirit helps us in our weakness. We do not know what we ought to pray for, but the Spirit himself intercedes for us with groans that words cannot express."

—ROMANS 8:26

Today read through the Scripture passages and pray and journal as you ask for God's restoration of your heart. This is a day to reflect on all the things that have been revealed to you about your heart, to turn to God and give yourself over to him so that he can transform you, and to commit yourself to being his servant.

A Prayer of Repentance

Begin with a short prayer to God, asking that he would open your heart to his restoration.

Think back to the first week of reading, and ponder the things you identified that were holding you back from answering God's call to love and serve the poor.

Consider how your material wealth has affected your compassion for those in need. Ask God to reveal to you the ways your material wealth has prevented you from loving the poor. Write your reflections here.

Now pray through the things you wrote down. Tell God you want to turn away from these things, and ask for his help in doing so.

Consider how your lifestyle has affected your compassion for those in need. Has busyness, individualism, or thinking of yourself first prevented you from loving the poor? Write your reflections here.

Now pray through the things you wrote down. Tell God you want to turn away from these things, and ask for his help in doing so.

Have you allowed yourself to become numb to the needs of this world, allowing yourself to not really get involved or be informed? Write your reflections here.

Now pray through the things you wrote down. Tell God you want to turn away from these things, and ask for his help in doing so.

Pray through Psalm 51:1-12 (on following page).

Have mercy on me, O God,

according to your unfailing love;

according to your great compassion

blot out my transgressions.

Wash away all my iniquity

and cleanse me from my sin...

Let me hear joy and gladness;

let the bones you have crushed rejoice.

Hide your face from my sins

and blot out all my iniquity.

Create in me a pure heart, O God,

and renew a steadfast spirit within me.

Do not cast me from your presence

or take your Holy Spirit from me.

Restore to me the joy of your salvation

and grant me a willing spirit, to sustain me.

—Psalm 51:1-12

Write your prayer of repentance here. Confess what
you've allowed to stop your compassion, and commit to
turn away from these things. Ask God to change and
restore your heart, and thank him for his grace.

A Prayer of Hope

Read through Isaiah 58:8-12, God's promises to Israel when the people help those in need:

Then your light will break forth like the dawn,
and your healing will quickly appear;
then your righteousness will go before you,
and the glory of the Lord will be your rear guard.
Then you will call, and the Lord will answer;
you will cry for help, and he will say: Here am I.

If you do away with the yoke of oppression,
with the pointing finger and malicious talk,
and if you spend yourselves in behalf of the hungry
and satisfy the needs of the oppressed,
then your light will rise in the darkness,
and your night will become like the noonday.

The Lord will guide you always;
he will satisfy your needs in a sun-scorched land
and will strengthen your frame.
You will be like a well-watered garden,
like a spring whose waters never fail.

Your people will rebuild the ancient ruins
and will raise up the age-old foundations;
you will be called Repairer of Broken Walls,
Restorer of Streets with Dwellings.

—Isaiah 58:8–12

Do you think there is a promise for you in this passage? Is there a particular verse that grabs you about how God may bless you when you answer his call? Underline this verse or line.

Write your thoughts about it here.

Do you have hope for what God has for you and for this world? Does the passage in Isaiah give you hope? How? Write your thoughts here about God's hope.

Say or write a prayer of thanks to God for his promises. Thank him for wanting not only to restore you, but also to use you to be a restorer. Ask God to fill you with his hope for this world and for your part in it.

A Prayer of Commitment

Think back to all of the verses you read in the
second week regarding helping those in need.
Was there one verse or passage that really stood
out to you and convicted you? Write it here:

Write why this Scripture affected you, and what
you think it may mean for your actions.

Based on how the Holy Spirit nudged your heart
through Scripture, what do you think God has in
store for you? Write here your commitment to God
in answering his call to you to be a restorer
in this world.

*End with a prayer of thanks to God. Praise God for his compassion. Thank God for
the way he restores your heart and wants to use you in this world.*

"Let justice roll on like a river, righteousness like a never-failing stream!"

—AMOS 5:24

Today, read through the Scripture passages and pray and journal as you ask God to prepare your heart for what he has in store for you. This day, you'll look ahead to the good works God has for you and ask his blessing in answering his call.

A Prayer of Thanks and Praise

Begin with a prayer of praise to God. Write here a list of his characteristics that you praise him for.

Thank God for the journey he has taken you on and the ways he has changed your heart. Write here the things you're thankful he has done in your heart.

A Prayer of Preparation

Now go back and read the commitment you wrote yesterday. Pray through it, and recommit it to God.

Read Acts 17:26-27 and Ephesians 2:10.

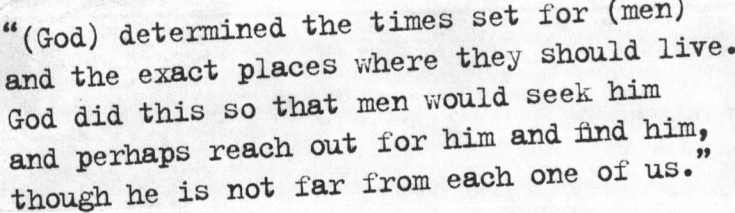

"(God) determined the times set for (men) and the exact places where they should live. God did this so that men would seek him and perhaps reach out for him and find him, though he is not far from each one of us."

—ACTS 17:26-27

"We are God's workmanship, created in Christ Jesus to do good works, which God prepared in advance for us to do."

—EPHESIANS 2:10

Why do you believe God placed you where he did? What good works do you think he may have prepared for you to do? Reflect on this and pray that God would show you why he has placed you exactly where he has. Write your thoughts and prayer here.

Read Psalm 25:1-5 as a reminder that our hope and trust are in God.

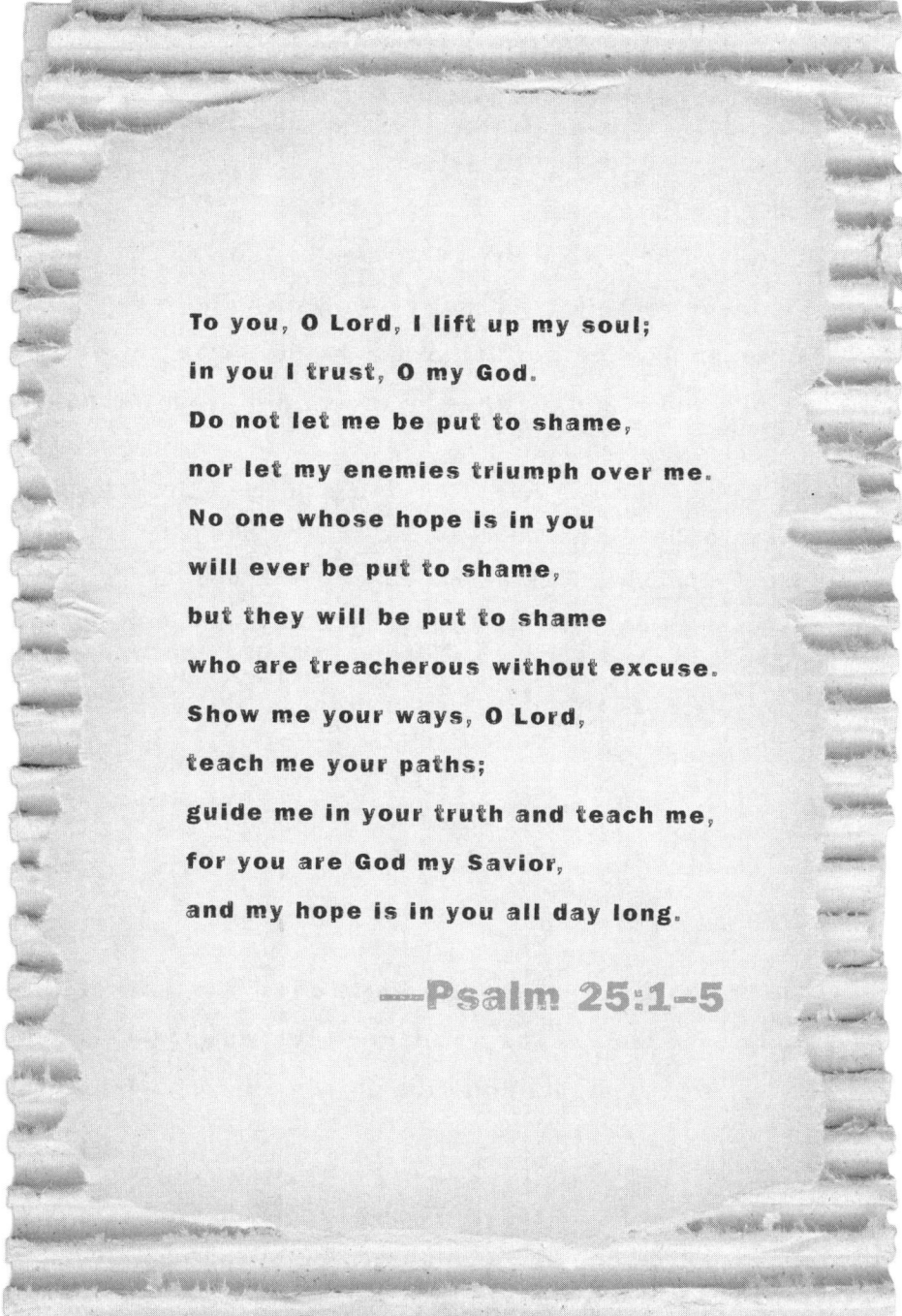

To you, O Lord, I lift up my soul;

in you I trust, O my God.

Do not let me be put to shame,

nor let my enemies triumph over me.

No one whose hope is in you

will ever be put to shame,

but they will be put to shame

who are treacherous without excuse.

Show me your ways, O Lord,

teach me your paths;

guide me in your truth and teach me,

for you are God my Savior,

and my hope is in you all day long.

—Psalm 25:1-5

Pray that God would fill you with his hope for this world, and pray to put your trust only in him.

Read Ephesians 1:18-20.

Know the hope to which (God) has called you . . . and his incomparably great power for us who believe. That power is like the working of his mighty strength, which he exerted in Christ when he raised him from the dead.

Pray that God will fill you with his Holy Spirit so you might have the hope to which God has called you and his incomparably great power. Ask God to help you to rely only on his power and hope in serving others, not on your own.

Read 2 Corinthians 10:3-4.

We do not wage war as the world does. The weapons we fight with are not the weapons of the world. On the contrary, they have divine power to demolish strongholds.

Pray that God would use you to demolish strongholds. Pray also that God would protect you in the spiritual battle that is raging in this world.

Read 1 Corinthians 13:3-7.

If I give all I possess to the poor and surrender my body to the flames, but have not love, I gain nothing. Love is patient, love is kind. It does not envy, it does not boast, it is not proud. It is not rude, it is not self-seeking, it is not easily angered, it keeps no record of wrongs. Love does not delight in evil but rejoices with the truth. It always protects, always trusts, always hopes, always perseveres.

Pray that God would fill you with his love, that it would be your banner and your motivator in serving others.

To close, pray Matthew 6:9-10.

Our Father in heaven, hallowed be your name, your kingdom come, your will be done on earth as it is in heaven.

Week Four
Reflection Questions

What challenged or inspired you most in this week's reading?

Do you agree that prayer is the "real" work we're called to as Christians? Why or why not?

How do you most like to approach God in prayer? In what way do you want to make prayer more of a daily habit?

How have you seen God act through prayer in the past? Do you believe that God will work through your prayers for this world? Why or why not?

Action Steps

1. If you're reading this book with a group, have a time of prayer together, dedicating yourselves to God and committing yourselves to obey his commands to love those in need.

2. Reread all of the journal pages you've written so far in the book. Reflect on and pray through what you wrote.

3. Next week, you'll explore how you can commit more specifically to helping others. Consider fasting on Day 23 or 24 to prepare for this.

4. Reread what you wrote on Day 18 regarding making prayer a habit—and start doing what you wrote down!

5. Talk to a friend or family member about what you're excited about—how God is working in you and changing you to be more like him.

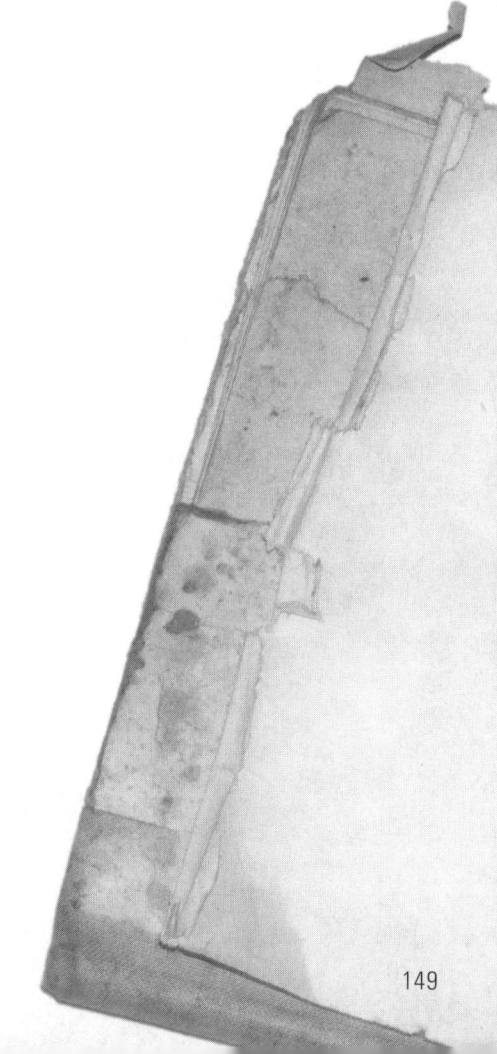

Be the
CHANGE

THE JOURNEY OF SERVING those in need is, in essence, the journey of

following Christ. And God has created each person uniquely for the journey,

giving each one spiritual gifts, skills, and passions with which to serve him, to be

the change we want to see in the world. This week we'll explore our individual

gifts and be reminded that it is God's grace that sustains us along the way.

HOPE LIVES

Be the change that you want to see in the world.

DAY 21: BE THE CHANGE

"Be the change that you want to see in the world."
—MOHANDAS GANDHI

God has been weaving a story throughout this journey. Looking back, I see that it truly has been a journey guided by God. I started by asking a lot of questions: "What is keeping me from helping others?" "What does the Bible say about it?" "What can I start doing to help others?" I've awakened to my sometime numbness, my hyper-individualism, and my material wealth. I've become convinced through Scripture of God's strong desire for me to help those in need. I've learned so much about what poverty is and how I can help combat it. But now I'm realizing there is so much more to the journey. God has drawn me along on this journey not just to learn about those things—he has drawn me along to get my heart.

What God always wanted was my heart; he wants a relationship with me. God wants me to know him. All those Bible verses on serving those in need aren't just God's list of do's and don'ts intended to transform me into a good person. Those verses reveal God's heart for this world—his awing love and compassion. God loves me, and he wants me to follow him. And when I follow Christ, God's love and compassion become *my* heart, too. God's Holy Spirit transforms me so that compassion is an overflow from my heart. Compassion isn't about checking off my charity box twice a year on my Christian to-do list. Compassion is who I am—through God's grace and by his Spirit. Every day. In every interaction. With every breath.

Be the Change

It's like Gandhi's famous quote: "*Be* the change." It's not "*do* the change." God wants my heart, not just my actions. God wants me to be who he created me to be. And now that I realize this isn't just about doing something, I think *I am* ready to do something. God created me in a very particular way, and he has very particular good works planned for me. As it says in Ephesians 4:11-13, God created me as he did "for works of service" so that I might attain "the whole measure of the fullness of Christ." When

I use the way I was created to serve God, I'll attain more of the fullness of Christ—I'll become more like him. So what is the change God wants me to "be" for this world? I think God can reveal this through my spiritual gifts, my skills, and my heart.

Spiritual Gifts

The New Testament reveals that God has given each individual in the body of Christ a spiritual gift with which to serve others. When we each use our gifts in concert, we become a full, functioning body, able to react to all the needs of those around us. Here are some of the gifts God gives.

"It was he who gave some to be **apostles,** some to be **prophets,** some to be **evangelists,** and some to be **pastors** and **teachers,** *to prepare God's people for works of service,* so that the body of Christ may be built up until we all reach unity in the faith and in the knowledge of the Son of God and become mature, attaining to the whole measure of the fullness of Christ."

—Ephesians 4:11-13,
(emphasis added)

"We have different gifts, according to the grace given us. If a man's gift is **prophesying,** let him use it in proportion to his faith. If it is **serving,** let him serve; if it is **teaching,** let him teach; if it is **encouraging,** let him encourage; if it is **contributing to the needs of others,** let him give generously; if it is **leadership,** let him govern diligently; if it is **showing mercy,** let him do it cheerfully."

—Romans 12:6-8

"Now to each one the manifestation of the Spirit is given for the common good. To one there is given through the Spirit **the message of wisdom**, to another **the message of knowledge** by means of the same Spirit, to another **faith** by the same Spirit, to another **gifts of healing** by that one Spirit, to another **miraculous powers**, to another **prophecy**, to another **distinguishing between spirits**, to another **speaking in different kinds of tongues**, and to still another the **interpretation of tongues**."

—1 Corinthians 12:7-10

"Now you are the body of Christ, and each one of you is a part of it. And in the church God has appointed first of all **apostles**, second **prophets**, third **teachers**, then **workers of miracles**, also **those having gifts of healing, those able to help others, those with gifts of administration,** and **those speaking in different kinds of tongues**."

—1 Corinthians 12:27-28

These are gifts God gave us to serve one another, the church. But doesn't it follow that these gifts would also be the way we'd each be most effective serving everyone around us and the world in general?

There are *apostles, prophets, evangelists, pastors, teachers, servers, encouragers, givers, leaders,* and *mercy showers.* There are *those with the message of wisdom, the message of knowledge, the gift of faith, the gift of healing, the gift of distinguishing between spirits, the gift of speaking in different tongues,* and *the gift of interpretation of tongues.* There are *workers of miracles, those able to help others,* and *those with gifts of administration.*

As I read these gifts, it's easy for me to see the gifts I don't have. Sadly, I'm not actually that great at showing mercy. (If someone falls down, I'm probably going to be the last on the scene with a bandage and empathetic tears.) But I am great at encouraging—I love to see and encourage the potential in others. I won't ever serve by becoming a field nurse. But I can serve by sharing God's encouragement with people who need to believe God's truth about themselves. When I lived in Amsterdam, my roommate Leslie had the gift of faith—she was amazing at believing God would do huge things for those in need and devoting herself to pray for them. My father-in-law has the gift of giving—he gives his money (and his time, working as a doctor) to help those in need. My friend Jackie has the gift of administration, and she uses it to organize food drives and mission trips and visits to shelters.

Skills

Besides our gifts, God has also given us particular skills that can determine how we can best serve others. I have a friend, Dave, who is a remarkable persuader. He uses this skill to speak up for the helpless, to persuade others to serve children in poverty around the world. I know others who are lawyers, doctors, bankers, homebuilders, and accountants who use their professional skills to help out those in need through volunteering or discounted services. Others are great cooks who prepare meals for families in a tight spot. I have the skill of writing, and I can use this skill, along with my gift of encouragement, to correspond with children in poverty who need love and encouragement.

Heart

In addition to our gifts and skills, a third factor guides our actions—our hearts. God created all people with unique passions, things they feel so strongly about that they want to pour all their energy into those things. God will give some people hearts for serving children, others hearts for serving the elderly. One person may have a heart for a particular country; another may have a heart for a particular cause. My friend Ned has a heart for those on the margins of society, the misfits. His heart nudges him to reach out to those who the rest of society might overlook or pass by and to become their friend and encourager. My friend Jen has a passion for travel. She directs this passion into mission trips, to help build homes for the poor and encourage churches in other countries. I have another friend, Kate, who has a passion for social justice, so she enrolled in law school to serve God through her profession. Through my experiences, God has given me a heart for women and children exploited by the sex trade, and I want to use my voice and actions to speak up for them.

God has placed a desire for change in our hearts—a change that we're passionate to see in this world, whether it's the acceptance of misfits, hospitality for the hungry, or justice for children. This was part of God's planning when he created good works for us in advance. How amazing! How kind! God has created each of us so that we can, as Gandhi said, "be the change that [we] want to see in the world."

Reflect on the past several weeks and consider the ways God has used those weeks to change your heart. Write down some of the steps of your journey.

MY PRAYER

Dear Lord, I thank you that you began this journey with me. It's your grace that has been guiding me. Use your Holy Spirit to transform me so that I have your heart. I want to know you more, and I thank you that in serving others I can draw closer to you. Help me to find the good works you have prepared in advance for me.

DAY 22: PRESSED DOWN, SHAKEN TOGETHER, AND RUNNING OVER

"Give, and it will be given to you.
A good measure, pressed down, shaken together and
running over, will be poured into your lap.
For with the measure you use, it will be measured to you."
—LUKE 6:38

My friend Dave DeBruine is a good example to me of "[loving] each other deeply, [using] whatever gift he has received to serve others" (1 Peter 4:8-10). He uses the gifts, skills, and heart God has given him to be an advocate for children on behalf of Compassion International, committing himself to finding caring sponsors for children in poverty around the world. I sat with him on a hot August night, eating ice cream cones, as he told me his story. This is what he had to say.

I took a trip to El Salvador in 1993 that changed my life. I had become a sponsor of a girl from El Salvador named Yolanda in 1991. I did it for the wrong reason—guilt—but even when we do something for the wrong reason, God can turn it around for good. I decided to visit El Salvador because it sounded cool; no one I knew had ever been there. Again, God used my bad motivation for good.

That trip changed me. Seeing poverty ripped my heart out. I had heard about it; I thought I understood it. But when you're standing there, meeting real kids who might not have eaten that day, it's overwhelming. I didn't understand it then, but every time I'd open my mouth, I'd cry. It's not acceptable in our society for a guy to cry, but I realized that God had revealed his heart for the poor to me—how he weeps over the poor. When I got back, I wanted to forget it all. I tried to get busy with work, but I couldn't deny what happened or the way I felt. I was given the opportunity to become an advocate, and I finally gave in.

Now I'm an advocate for Compassion International and find sponsors for children in poverty. The joy of helping children is overwhelming. Nights when I work at an event and many children find sponsors, I could fly home—I wouldn't even need a car. It really hits me that there are children God loves immensely, whose lives are changed because people are willing to give. God says in the Bible that if you give, he'll give it back, packed down and overflowing. That's what God has done for me. I can't imagine my life without serving these children. The joy and peace God gives me while serving is incredible.

I went on a trip to Guatemala to visit children sponsored through Compassion. I was working a lot before the trip and barely had time to pack before my flight. As I got off the plane, I realized I didn't bring anything for the kids—no candy or footballs or jump-ropes. I prayed, "Lord, please let the love you've given me be enough." There was this awkward moment when we arrived at the project—you're never quite sure how to interact with the kids. Finally, I grabbed a kid and put him on my shoulders. It was either going to be great or awful. He loved it and laughed. Next thing I knew, I was a human jungle gym with kids climbing up my arms and legs. There was a 3-year-old boy who ran up and tugged my pants and ran off. I chased him and threw him in the air, and he'd laugh. Then he'd do it again—for an hour. The joy in my heart—I thought I might explode. The love God had given me was enough. To spend this day playing with a little boy in poverty, making him feel special and loved—doing something anyone could do—was incredible.

I was hot and tired, and sat down to rest. While I caught my breath, I looked up and saw the fence around the project. Hanging on the fence were all of the children from the neighborhood. They came hearing the laughter and joy, and they were peering over the fence. All I could see in their faces was "Why not me?" I wanted to bring them all in. That's why I'm an advocate for children. When I speak to people, my question is, "Will you bring one more child in and off that fence?"

It's tough to think about the children on that fence, who live in grim situations sometimes without hope, but I often come back to it as motivation when it'd be nice to do something else. I know if I give up a day I'd spend on myself, it may mean one or five or 100 kids are off the fence. What greater gift is there? What better way can I spend my time? There are times I drive down the street and see expensive cars and homes. But if getting those things meant working more and volunteering less, it's not worth it. I wouldn't give up anything in exchange for this ministry. It's isn't always easy, but it's priceless.

My life is nothing close to perfect, and I struggle like everyone. I don't feel qualified to speak up for these children. But it's pretty exciting to be given that responsibility and gift. God blesses my service. The time I give is just one link in a chain of events that will help children see God's love for them and lead them to a relationship with Christ. The actions we take are pebbles that hit the water and make ripples. Children escape poverty through sponsorship; they accept Christ through sponsorship, and it makes ripples—parents and neighbors come to Christ. Fathers give up drinking. It's exciting to hear all the stories. I don't know the future of the children I sponsor, but God does. I do what I do out of faith that God will change that life. Not all will have a fairy-tale ending, but that isn't what I'm called to. I'm not called to solve all the problems on my own. I'm called to be obedient to what God has said in the Bible. I step out in faith, and God will take care of the rest.

I didn't ever expect that when I served I'd feel so alive. I feel more alive and on fire when I'm serving than at any point in my life. When I'm serving, I get to be who God created me to be. Without a shadow of a doubt, this is why I'm on the earth—to serve these children. I never thought when I started as a sponsor I would discover my greatest purpose. Nothing feels more right. Nothing feels better. That was such a surprise—I had no idea that's what God had in store for me. But when you do what God calls you to do, you know. All the puzzle pieces come together, and you don't want to do anything but that. It's like having a piece of heaven on earth.

Here on earth, I'll never see the impact of the ministry God has blessed me with, but one of the most blessed moments of my life was when I visited El Salvador with my mom. We visited a project that put on a skit for us. They were looking for a volunteer, and I volunteered, thinking I was going to be an actor in the skit. The children brought out a chair and played Ray Boltz's song "Thank You." They acted out the song, thanking me for giving to the Lord. To have children singing to me, thanking me for what I've done, saying there will be people in heaven thanking me—how do I have the right to be blessed in that way?

At another project in El Salvador, we got off the bus and went in the church. As my mom and I stepped in, the church erupted in a five-minute standing ovation. I leaned over to my mom and said, "I don't deserve this. All I do is write a check once a month." Many of us dream of making a touchdown in the Super Bowl or doing something the world deems fantastic. But in a way I think I've scored a touchdown—for God. If I had my choice of serving a child that will someday be in heaven or scoring a touchdown in the Super Bowl, I'd take the kid any day.

The greatest joy I've experienced in my ministry to the poor is in the small things. I sponsor a boy named Edgar in Ecuador. Edgar's mother died in childbirth several years ago, along with the baby. Edgar's father, José, had to have surgery and give up his job. Hospital bills came for his mother's care and his father's surgery, and the family had no money. So José sold their animals to pay the hospital bills. In three months, Edgar had lost his mom, the baby, his dad's health, and their livestock. They were devastated.

When I found out, I thought, "I've got to do something." I was able to send them a family gift of $300, and they were able to buy a cow. When I got the letter with a picture of that cow, it was incredible. The cow has since had a calf and is producing milk for the kids to drink. They're selling the extra milk, and they'll raise the calf. The cow will produce another calf each year, and after a couple of years, they'll be able to start selling the calves. José makes $300 a year currently. In the future, he'll be able to sell a cow for $150. If he sells two calves, he can double his income. My small gift made a huge impact, a sustainable impact.

My screen saver on my computer at work is Edgar and his family with the cow. It's pretty cool that now Edgar and his brother are able to drink milk because of something so small that I did. It's in the little things like that that God gives me joy—Edgar and his cow, that 3-year-old I chased in Guatemala. God continues to bless me in so many ways. He has given me "a good measure, pressed down, shaken together and running over."

In My Own Words

Write about a time you served others and God used the experience to bring you joy.

Do you agree that we find our purpose when we're doing what we were created to do: to serve others? Have you ever found your purpose in serving others? How?

M Y   P R A Y E R

Dear Lord, I praise you that you want to give me a life with purpose and filled with joy and peace. I want to find my peace in serving you. I want to know your joy through serving others. I give myself to you to be the person you created me to be and to do the things you prepared me to do. Please help me to be your faithful servant.

DAY 23: USING YOUR GIFTS

"Above all, love each other deeply . . . Each one should use whatever gift he has received to serve others, faithfully administering God's grace in its various forms. If anyone speaks, he should do it as one speaking the very words of God. If anyone serves, he should do it with the strength God provides, so that in all things God may be praised through Jesus Christ."

—1 PETER 4:8-11

"For you created my inmost being; you knit me together in my mother's womb. I praise you because I am fearfully and wonderfully made; your works are wonderful, I know that full well."

—PSALM 139:13-14

It's so exciting to be part of God's plan to love and serve others. For Dave, it was a matter of finding his purpose in life. That's pretty cool! Today take some time to journal and pray about your spiritual gifts to explore how you can serve others. Spiritual gifts are special abilities God gives to each Christian through the Holy Spirit to share God's love with others and strengthen the body of Christ. God doesn't ask us to serve the poor and then leave us unequipped to do it—he gives us exactly what we need to help, bless, and serve others.

If you've never taken a spiritual-gifts inventory before, you may want to take one to help identify your gift. (You can find inventories online by searching "spiritual gifts test.") However, taking an inventory isn't necessary to find out how God has gifted you to serve—the early church didn't have inventories! Paul Ford, author of *Discovering Your Ministry Identity,* says, "We do not have to go to school to learn how to serve Him. Our service grows out of who we already are. His grace has already fitted us with tools for the Kingdom of God." He says our gifts are "not what you do for God, but who you already are in Christ." Pray that God and the Holy Spirit will reveal to you how he has gifted you to serve. If you're not sure what your spiritual gifts are, try serving in various roles to see which bring the greatest results for God and the greatest fulfillment for you.

Digging In

Start by praying. Thank God for creating you wonderfully and uniquely. Ask the Holy Spirit to fill you and guide you as you consider your spiritual gifts. Ask God to reveal to you ways that he has gifted you to serve.

Think back to a time you served others—in any capacity—and it felt just great and great results were achieved for God. It could have been organizing an event, encouraging a sick person, leading a mission trip, serving a meal, sharing a Bible passage with someone, cleaning up after church, casting a vision for a ministry. Write about that experience here.

Flip back to yesterday's reading and reread the passages that list the spiritual gifts.

Then read this brief explanation of each spiritual gift.

Apostles: *Apostle* literally means "one sent on a mission." Apostles have the gift of building spiritual foundations, expanding ministries, and planting churches.

Prophecy: The gift of speaking forth the present and future truth of God.

Evangelism: The gift of sharing the gospel of Jesus Christ with others.

Pastoring: The gift of protecting, spiritually guiding, and caring for the body of Christ.

Teaching: The gift of communicating and instructing others in the truths of the Bible.

Service: The gift of identifying the needs of others and doing whatever it takes to meet them.

Encouragement: The gift of coming alongside someone to comfort, challenge, and encourage.

Giving: The gift of giving material resources freely and cheerfully for the sake of others.

Leadership: The gift of providing vision and direction for the church.

Mercy: The gift of empathizing, assisting, and showing compassion to those who suffer physically, mentally, or emotionally.

Helps: The gift of unselfishly meeting the needs of others to free them up for service.

Administration: The gift of planning, organizing, and supervising others, carrying out the ministry goals of the church.

The Message of Wisdom: The gift of applying wisdom to life, giving wise spiritual counsel for decision making and daily life circumstances.

The Message of Knowledge: The gift of seeking out, understanding, and sharing insight into biblical knowledge.

Faith: The gift of trusting God with confidence, being persuaded of God's power and promises to achieve his will.

Healing: The gift of restoring physical, mental, emotional, and spiritual health to an individual.

Distinguishing Between Spirits: The gift of determining whether the source of a behavior or action is God, man, or Satan.

Speaking in/Interpretation of Tongues: The gift of the Holy Spirit enabling one to speak in a language unknown to the speaker; the Holy Spirit enabling one to interpret the words of one speaking in tongues to build up the church.

Miracles: The gift of performing deeds for which divine intervention is the only explanation, bringing glory to God.

After reading the list, write here the gifts that jump out at you—things that you feel God has given you. It could be just one gift or it could be several.

Write why you think you might have each gift. Is it a particular experience you had, is it something you just love to do, is it something you think is of utmost importance?

Brainstorming

Now take some time to reflect, pray about, and brainstorm how you might use these gifts. You can choose the top gift you might have, or you can brainstorm for several gifts.

Brainstorm ways you could serve your church, the body of Christ, using this spiritual gift. These don't have to be specifically focused on serving the poor, but on serving the church. This exercise will help you get an idea of how you're effective serving in general.

Now write some needs in your local community. Think of people on the margins of society: the poor, widows, orphans, and foreigners. Is there a particular group, a particular person, or a particular need in your community that you could serve? Do you have a heart for a particular group?

Now brainstorm ways you could serve those in need
in your community with your spiritual gift. If your
gift is encouragement, you could bring cookies and
a welcome to international graduate students (who
may be quite lonely!). If your gift is the message
of wisdom, it may be to speak out on behalf of those
in need in your community. If your gift is mercy,
it could be serving at a local shelter. If your
gift is leadership, it may be envisioning a ministry
that your community is currently lacking. Try to be
specific, and don't be afraid to be creative! Think
big—dream of how God can use you. But also think
small—God can bless and use even the smallest of
actions!

Now think on a global scale. How can you use your
spiritual gifts to serve those around the world in
need? If you have the gift of faith, you could use
your gift to pray for big things. If you have the
gift of service, you may be a great candidate for
a short-term mission trip. If you have the gift of
administration, you might want to help plan that
mission trip. If you have the gift of giving, think
of ways to give cheerfully and abundantly. If you
have the gift of prophecy, speak out to persuade
others to join you in serving.

Pray and be creative. Write your ideas here.

Take your brainstorming further by researching organizations that are already serving the people you think you may want to serve and that can use your particular gifts. Read through the list of organizations at the end of the book, or research organizations online and at www.charitynavigator.com.

Close by praying, committing your ideas to God. Pray that God will guide you in selflessly, eagerly, and liberally serving others. Pray that he will help make his purpose known to you.

MY PRAYER

Dear Lord, I praise you for how you made this world—that each person has a unique gift and purpose. Thank you for making me who I am. Thank you for equipping me to serve you in a special way. Use your Holy Spirit to guide me in using my spiritual gifts to serve you. I give myself to you. I want to be used by you to be a blessing to those around me.

> "Trust in the Lord and do good . . . Delight yourself in the
> Lord and he will give you the desires of your heart.
> Commit your way to the Lord; trust in him and he will do this:
> He will make your righteousness shine like the dawn,
> the justice of your cause like the noonday sun."
>
> —PSALM 37:3-6

Not only do we have particular gifts to serve others with; God has also given us skills and passions. Today, spend time journaling and praying about your skills and your heart, finding how God can use you to serve others in a way made just for you.

Begin by praying. Thank God for the way he made you and his special purpose for you. Pray that God's Holy Spirit will reveal to you the skills and heart you've been given to serve others.

Skills

Our skills can help us find ways we can uniquely serve others. A skill can be your profession, a hobby, or an aptitude. It could be something you learned in school, something you're naturally good at, or something you have a lot of experience in. It could be finances, designing, cooking, influencing, analyzing, knitting, writing, doctoring, speaking, repairing, strategizing, building, gardening, listening, engineering, and on and on.

Write here your top skills, the things you're good at and the things you like to do.

Now brainstorm ways you can use these skills to serve
others in your church and local community. If you're
skilled in repair, you could volunteer with Habitat for
Humanity. If you're skilled in listening, you could
volunteer at after-school programs or shelters. If you're
skilled at finances, you could offer financial counseling
to those who may need it. If you're skilled at knitting,
you could donate warm garments you've made. These ideas
can be big or small in scope. Write your ideas here.

Now brainstorm ways you can use these skills to serve those
in need around the world. If you're skilled in building,
you could use your skill to help rebuild churches abroad
after disasters. If you enjoy writing, you could use your
skill to write letters to encourage churches or individuals
abroad. If you're a great baker, you could organize a bake
sale to raise money. If you're a great influencer, you could
write letters to politicians for a cause or take up grant
writing. Write your ideas here.

Heart

Each person has been given different passions from God. Many times, our passions derive from our personal experiences—something that has affected us deeply in the past or something we've suffered through or watched someone else suffer through. Or it could be certain people we've had experience with. Or places that just really intrigue us. Some people just love kids and have a heart to speak up for them. Some people have known someone with AIDS and have a heart to fight the disease. Other people may just love traveling or love Asian culture (and food!). Others may have had a relative with a disability and have a heart for others with disabilities.

Consider different groups of people. Is there a certain group you feel passionate about serving, such as single mothers, children, teenage boys, the elderly, widows, orphans, internationals, or those with physical disabilities? It could be anyone. Write here who you think you may be passionate about serving.

Now think through causes. Is there a particular issue or need in the world that grabs at your heart, the thing that you'd say, "If I could get involved in any one cause, that'd be it"? It might be child labor or health education or international trade. Write your ideas here.

Consider other passions you might have—maybe you're passionate about traveling or Indian culture or motorcycles or art or reading. Write here what general, miscellaneous passions you have in life.

Review the answers you wrote down for your heart. Do any really jump out at you? Can you see yourself investing in one to serve others in some way? Write the top few things here and ideas for how you could get involved in these passions to serve others. If you love running and have a heart for those with disabilities, find organizations to partner with in races. If you love biking and have a heart for inner-city kids, join a mentoring organization and use biking to build a relationship with the child you're mentoring. If you love cooking Indian food, start an international meal club where you share meals with friends and also donate meals to those in need.

Review what you wrote yesterday about your spiritual
gifts. Then reread what you wrote about your skills and
passions. What stands out? Do you see any synthesis
between these three things? Is there an idea that can
combine your gifts, skills, and heart? For example, I
have the gift of teaching, I have the skill of writing,
and I have a heart for those in poverty...so I wrote
this book. Creatively mix and match your ideas for your
gifts, skills, and heart. Write down the ideas that
really capture your heart and use your gifts and skills.

Spend time praying to determine how you can start loving and serving others. (If you don't have a lot of time today, set aside more time on another day to earnestly pray about these ideas.) Pray right now to commit these ideas to God and ask for the Holy Spirit's guidance.

MY PRAYER

Dear Lord, I thank you for the skills and passions you've given me. I thank you that I can use things I'm excited about and am good at to serve you. I thank you for giving me spiritual gifts so I can serve others in a unique and powerful way. I commit all these ideas to you. Please guide me in determining how I can share your love with others. I praise you for your grace and compassion for me and for this world!

DAY 25: A LIFE OF GRACE

"Let us not become weary in doing good, for at the proper time we will reap a harvest if we do not give up."

—GALATIANS 6:9

"To prepare God's people for works of service, so that the body of Christ may be built up until we all reach unity in the faith and in the knowledge of the Son of God and become mature, attaining to the whole measure of the fullness of Christ."

—EPHESIANS 4:12-13

Now that I've been on this journey with God for a little while, I can't help but look back and see what's different now from when I began. I'm struck that the difference isn't that I've started writing a check every month or begun volunteering so many hours each week or joined some philanthropic group. The change is in *me*. I'm a different person from who I was when I started on this road. I'm more awake to God's presence and deep love for everyone around me. I'm more awake to the people around me, more alert to their interests. It seems that God's great agenda for my life isn't that I take this or that particular action. It is that I am journeying closer to Christ and becoming more like him. As a wise woman I know once said, "It's not about *doing* something; it's about *being* something." As I become like Christ and begin to know him more, his love and service are an organic outflow of my life.

In Ephesians, Paul says that God's people were prepared for works of service so that they may attain the whole measure of the fullness of Christ. Everything is brought back to center. Attaining the fullness of Christ is the heart and the end of my journey. If I want to know Christ, I will serve and love others. As I do that, I get closer and closer to the fullness of Christ. He is always right beside me on the journey, but somehow his face becomes clearer and clearer with each step I take.

> " 'He defended the cause of the poor and needy...Is that not what it means to know me?' declares the Lord."
> —JEREMIAH 22:16

And, thank God, I'm not just powering my steps along on this journey with the strength of my own two legs. The vehicle in this journey is God's grace. I'm struck with the realization that this journey was never me—it didn't start with me and it's not compelled by me. God, in his grace, whispered to me and asked me on a journey. I'm here because God invited me along. I take missteps and stumble along the way, but it is God's grace that leads me.

> 'Tis grace has brought me safe thus far,
> And grace will lead me home.
> —JOHN NEWTON, "AMAZING GRACE"

It is God's grace and his Holy Spirit that are restoring me, slowly but surely, to the masterpiece he created me to be. His grace—not my own good intentions or good works—has brought me this far, and his grace will continue to guide me on the journey he has commissioned for me: to love and serve the world.

Knowing that God's grace is guiding me and his Holy Spirit is transforming me, how can I help but hope? It's not me alone and my half-baked dreams to change the world or my halfhearted attempts to make a difference.

It's God's world, God's will, God's hope.

I don't want to be part of a fad. It's so hot right now to be into Africa…into a cause… into the poor. What'll it be five years from now? I don't know, but I don't want a phase—I want Christ. I want to be on this road of serving Christ and walking beside him for the rest of my life—with his grace at the center, to keep me from growing "weary in doing good."

At the beginning of a journey, everything is new and exciting. I love an adventure. The freshness of it all keeps me striding forward each morning. But sooner or later, I'll have seen it all, heard it all. Routine will set in. And it will get hard. It may become a drudgery. And I'll become weary in doing good.

At these times in my journey (and I know myself well enough to know they will certainly come), I'll need to go back to the center: Christ and his grace and his hope. Along the path, I may pick up all those bad motivations I know I have: serving to feel good about myself, giving to assuage guilt, doing good for doing good's sake, acting to do something of great import. But when I misstep, God's grace is still there. God's Holy Spirit will nudge me to throw those motivations back down and remember the love and grace of Jesus Christ. Remember that a life of grace, a life of compassion, is the life of following Christ. It's the life in which I become who I was created to be.

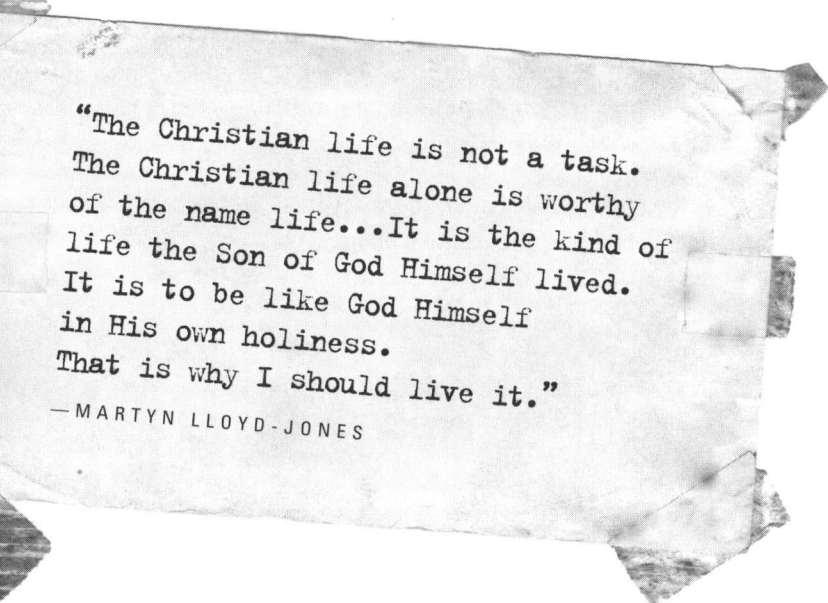

"The Christian life is not a task. The Christian life alone is worthy of the name life…It is the kind of life the Son of God Himself lived. It is to be like God Himself in His own holiness. That is why I should live it."

—MARTYN LLOYD-JONES

Hope Lives

Hope lives in me. Not because I've found some new strategy or organization for changing the world. Hope lives because the Lord is my hope.

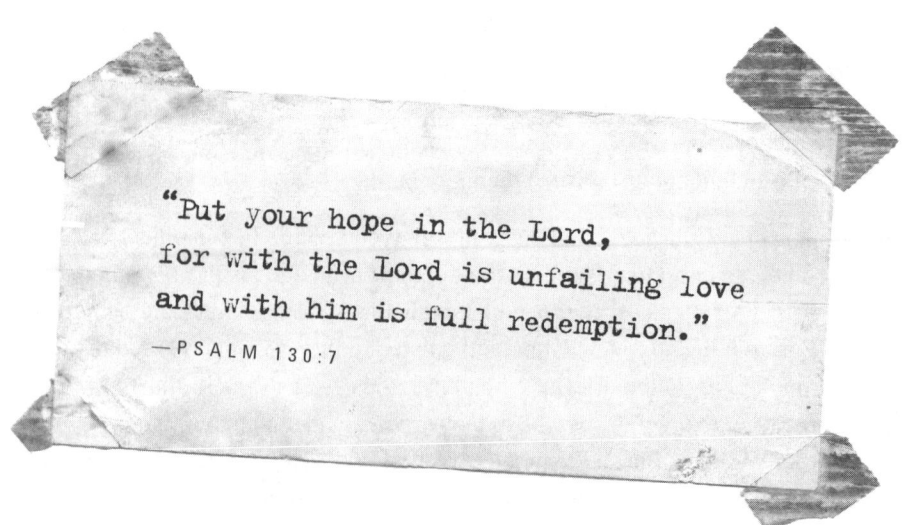

"Put your hope in the Lord,
for with the Lord is unfailing love
and with him is full redemption."
—PSALM 130:7

God's love for me is unfailing; God's love for this world is unfailing. He wants to bring me and this world to full redemption and restoration—to the whole measure of the fullness of Christ. My hope is in him. God's Holy Spirit is on the move to restore his treasures throughout this world. He's kindly asked me to be his companion on the journey—and I am one of the treasures he restores along the way.

At the end of the journey, I will hear Christ's words: "Well done, good and faithful servant! Come and share your master's happiness!"

"[The kingdom of heaven] will be like a man going on a journey, who called his servants and entrusted his property to them. To one he gave five talents of money...Then he went on his journey. The man who had received the five talents went at once and put his money to work and gained five more.

...After a long time the master of those servants returned and settled accounts with them. The man who had received the five talents brought the other five. 'Master,' he said, 'you entrusted me with five talents. See, I have gained five more.'

His master replied, 'Well done, good and faithful servant! You have been faithful with a few things; I will put you in charge of many things. Come and share your master's happiness!' "

—Matthew 25:14-21

Write your prayer. Thank God for the journey
you're on with him and for the Holy Spirit's
guidance for the rest of the journey as you
continue to attain the fullness of Christ.

My Prayer

Week Five
Reflection Questions

What have you discovered about the ways God may want to use you to serve others based on your spiritual gifts, skills, and heart?

Looking back on the past five weeks, how has God transformed you and restored you to the masterpiece he created you to be?

A life of grace and compassion is a way of life. How can you make sure it's not just a five-week "program," but a lasting lifestyle?

How is God's grace central in all of this?

Tell about the hope you have for God's will for yourself and this world.

Action Steps

1. Review your brainstorming on Days 23 and 24. Pray and commit to follow through on one (or two or three!) of the ways you brainstormed to love and serve others.

2. Review Week 4, in which you considered various ways to pray for others. Commit to one (or more!) of the ideas that you wrote down on Day 18 to devote yourself to prayer for others.

3. Before stepping out on the rest of your journey, spend an extended time in prayer with God (and with others if you're reading this book with a group). Commit yourself to the journey, and ask for God's blessing, grace, and peace as you serve him.

4. Talk to one person about how this journey has changed you. Share God's hope with others, and bring them along on the journey!

5. Research. If you're still looking for specific ways to get involved, do some research into ways to serve others in your church, in your community, and in the world. Following is a list of great organizations you might want to check out.

Organizations Through Which Hope Lives

Check out these organizations to see if one grabs your heart. Don't forget to visit www.charitynavigator.org to learn more about other charitable organizations.

Children's HopeChest responds to God's desire to create a world where every orphan knows God and experiences the blessings of family and acquires the skills necessary for independent life. www.hopechest.org

Compassion International is a Christian child-advocacy ministry that releases children from spiritual, physical, economic, and social poverty and enables them to become responsible, fulfilled Christian adults. www.compassion.com

Group Workcamps Foundation provides dynamic short-term mission trips, domestic and international. Since 1977, nearly a quarter of a million participants have grown in their relationship with Jesus, while providing more than 6 million hours of volunteer service directly to people in need. www.groupworkcamps.com

Habitat for Humanity is a Christian housing ministry that seeks to eliminate impoverished housing and homelessness from the world and to make decent shelter a matter of conscience and action. www.habitat.org

Healing Waters International works to reduce water-related illness and death in developing countries by building self-sustaining projects that make safe drinking water accessible to the poor and empowers local churches to bring physical, social, and spiritual healing to their communities. www.healingwatersintl.org

International Justice Mission is a human rights agency that rescues victims of violence, sexual exploitation, slavery, and oppression. IJM documents and monitors conditions of abuse and oppression, educates the church and public about the abuses, and mobilizes intervention on behalf of victims. www.ijm.org

The **Micah Challenge** is a global campaign to mobilize Christians against poverty. The campaign aims to deepen Christian engagement with impoverished and marginalized communities and to influence leaders of rich and poor nations to fulfill their promise to achieve the Millennium Development Goals to defeat poverty. www.themicahchallenge.org

ONE is a campaign to make poverty history, raising public awareness about the issues of global poverty, hunger, disease, and efforts to fight such problems in the world's poorest countries. www.one.org

Opportunity International provides emerging entrepreneurs with access to small loans and training that will enable them to start or expand their own businesses. www.opportunity.org

UNICEF, the United Nations Children's Fund, helps build a world where the rights of every child are realized. It influences decision makers and has a variety of partners at the grassroots level to turn innovative ideas into reality. www.unicef.org

NOTES

Produced in partnership with
Compassion International

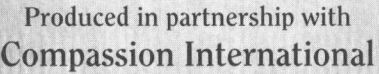

HOPE LIVES

A Journey of Restoration

Youth Ministry Kit

Take Your Youth on a Journey of Restoration

This five-session series helps your teenagers see beyond their own concerns and experience compassion for others. You'll get a leader guide and a DVD packed with discussion-sparking visual clips as well as a copy of the *Hope Lives* book.

ISBN 978-0-7644-3786-1 • $29.99

Produced in partnership with
Compassion International

HOPE LIVES
A Journey of Restoration

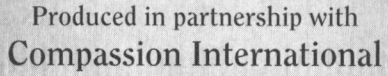

Small Group Kit
Take Your Small Group on a Journey of Restoration
Includes *Hope Lives* book and small-group DVD packed with interviews, questions, and effective discussion starters—guaranteed to spark conversation and compassion in small group members. A five-week study.
ISBN 978-0-7644-3785-4 • $29.99

Produced in partnership with
Compassion International

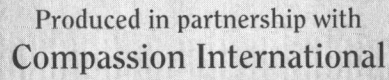

HOPE LIVES
A Journey of Restoration

Children's Ministry Kit

Take Your Children on a Journey of Restoration

Encourage kids to feel compassion for others! This five-week study sparks children to develop and demonstrate compassion. Includes leader guide with multi-age ideas to use in class, a worship music CD, and a *Hope Lives Prayer Ball* that will get kids talking and thinking about compassion. The result: changed lives!

ISBN 978-0-7644-3787-8 • $29.99

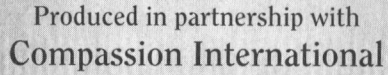

HOPE LIVES
A Journey of Restoration

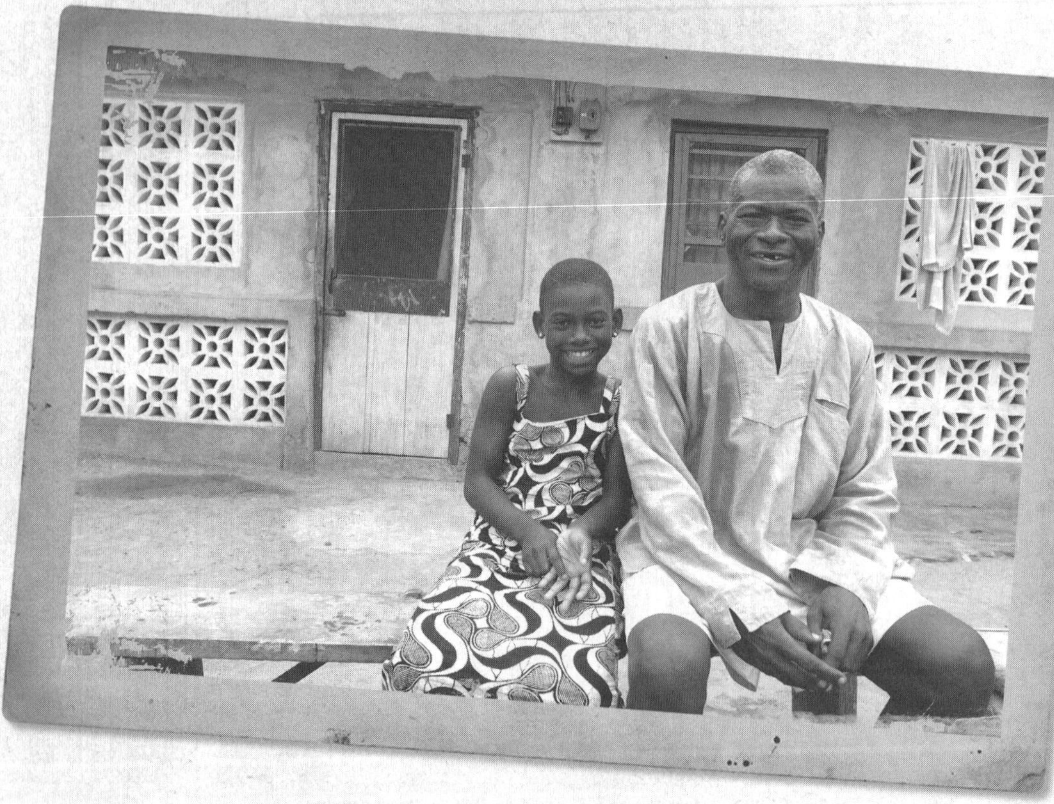

Pastor Kit

Take Your Church on a Journey of Restoration

Everything a pastor needs to launch a five-week all-church *Hope Lives* campaign, including a promotional video and other publicity pieces. Five messages supported by PowerPoint slides and video clips, as well as a copy of the *Hope Lives* book.

ISBN 978-0-7644-3784-7 • $49.99